In the Long Run

* * * *

"You don't have to be the best to accomplish the best.
Catch your dreams before they run away."

– Jordan Schilit

In the Long Run

Written for the High School Runner…

By a High School Runner

Jordan Schilit

JMS Publishing

2009

Jesuit "Tiger" logo courtesy of Jesuit High School.
Logo design by Michael Harris.

Copyright © 2009 by Jordan Schilit

1st printing. Printed in the United States of America

ISBN: 978-0-9841089-0-9
        0-9841089-0-4

Publisher: Jordan M. Schilit/JMS Publishing

Author/Publisher Information:
Jordan Schilit can be reached at:
jordan@schilit.net
813-601-RUNR
(813-601-7867)
http://www.freewebs.com/jordo1010/

Book Dedication

This book is first for my mom, who initially got me interested in running. Thanks for the opportunity to begin my racing career by finishing a 5K alongside you…in flip flops. I will always remember your favorite quote, "There will be days when I don't know if I can run a marathon. There will be a lifetime knowing that I did!"

Second, I would like to recognize my dad, who taught me the importance of demonstrating a combination of interior competitiveness and exterior modesty. Thanks for convincing me to keep running on the evening of October 13th, 2006. I wouldn't be half the person I am today if I hadn't decided to persevere in what I truly loved.

Contents

Preface and Acknowledgements

Since I was very young, my parents encouraged me to pursue an activity – any activity – that I loved. For some reason, while I was still in elementary school, I made the decision to start running cross country and track. Whether it was something my parents or friends told me directly, something they did to help me out, or simply some actions of others, I wanted to go out and prove my true capabilities as a runner.

A few years later, I began coming in first in my age group in a few local races and became more interested in the sport. I even got a chance to meet my cousin Matt Szylit from Melbourne, Australia, who represented his country as a distance runner in the Olympic Trials as well as the Maccabiah Games in Israel during the 1960s, and who encouraged me with my running. I was selected soon thereafter to represent my own country (the United States) at the 2005 Junior Maccabiah Games, where I met Coach Todd Wolin. He taught me how distance runners must eat from ALL food groups and get stronger in order to race at their full potential.

In middle school, I watched the Tampa Jesuit High School cross country team win a couple of state titles and dreamed that I would someday run for that team. I wanted to follow its winning ways and not only bring satisfaction to myself, but also to my teammates, my friends, and my family. I remember watching Andy Biladeau of Jesuit High School and Rolf Steier of nearby Berkeley Prep High School sweep awards at several big invitationals as well as their respective State Championship races. They, along with Coach Mike Boza and Coach Fred Steier, were mentors for me throughout my high school career, and encouraged my decision to apply to and enroll at Haverford College to continue my academic and athletic interests.

I have learned so much from all of my coaches throughout the years, starting from my first steps out on the track. Beginning with Randy Hall at the Hillel Day School and Coach Gary and his Tampa Trailblazers, I was always reminded to chase after the best, and never give up on my aspirations of competing with the state's elite.

Later on, I had the privilege of being mentored by one of the greatest high school coaches in the country – Coach Mike Boza of Tampa Jesuit High School – who taught me to be patient with my training and to appreciate that running is more focused on long-term goals, specifically an 8-10 year training plan. This approach not only helped me improve significantly, but helped Tampa Jesuit win 4 team State Championships over an 8 year span.

After Coach Boza's departure from Tampa Jesuit, Coach Greg Maurin emphasized spiritual reflection during our training. In essence, our performances should be for a greater good than merely for personal fulfillment. Coach David Revord taught me the importance of getting more turn-over and that speed training separates the men from the boys. He also reminded me of professional athletes that thrived under high pressure situations; my goal would be to take on that pressure and come through when my team needed me the most. Also, Coach Paul Williams taught me to be as tough as possible and that championships are won during the off-season – not during the races themselves.

Coach Ray Rodriguez, who was named Hillsborough County "Coach of the Year" for 2009, may have taught me one of the most important lessons – the value of sacrificing an individual championship in order to help the team prevail. I will never forget the final day of my high school running career - May 2nd, 2009. I am so thankful that on that day, I passed the ultimate test of selflessness by putting my Jesuit team ahead of my own personal goals, which was one of the most important milestones in my becoming an adult. Rather than drop out of the 1600m so that I could concentrate on winning a state title in my better event – the 3200m – I ran both of those distance races that day in order to maximize the points that my team could earn. The result was: state runner-up titles in the 1600m and the 3200m, to go along with a state championship (as well as a school record and the 6th best performance in the nation at that time) in the 4x800m relay, which gave our team the runner-up title in the state championship meet.

I was always hungry for more knowledge in the world of distance running. I even reached out to other coaches for advice, even Jesuit's rivals. I was amazed at the improvements that Coach McWilliams (Bishop Kenny), Coach Altimari

(Robinson), Coach Butler (Holy Trinity), Coach Steier (Berkeley Prep) and Coach Strack (Chamberlain), just to name a few, managed to create for their teams. For example, I remember Coach Strack telling me that he was happy to have 5 guys under 20:00 for 5K in 2007. Not only did every one of those guys PR in 2008, but the top-5 all managed to break 17:00 and took State Runner-Up honors at the Florida 3A State Finals.

I learned from the teams in Hillsborough County – Sickles, Robinson, Berkeley, Wharton, Chamberlain, Newsome, Leto, and Plant – and several powerhouses from around Florida -- such as Melbourne, Holy Trinity, Bishop Kenny, Belen Jesuit, Miami Columbus, Dr. Philips, and Leon. I will also never forget the encouragement of the many contributors to the Florida running community, such as Bob Cooke (Dr. Bob), Dan Howe, Dan Petrick, Andy Matthews, Frank Massari, Dror Vaknin, Jarret Slaven, Lynn Gray, and Jason Byrne.

And, I am thankful to the many training partners that have run the countless miles with me as we've shared great stories and memories, as well as encouragement for each other. First, I would like to thank my Jesuit teammates from the class of 2009: Connor, Connor, Logan, Ben Martin, Joe Pa, Mikey, Mac, and Tatro. Next, I am indebted to Jesuit cross country and track runners from years prior, including: Andy, A.B., Andrew, Ozzy, Scriv, Mike, Cade, John, Bennett, Hunter, Bracy, Hindman, and Sam. Also, I am thankful for meeting training partners from other teams in Hillsborough County, specifically: Derek Wehunt, Dan Wehunt, Bryan Gollins, Marc DeJute, Julian Gines, Jonathan Bermudez, Mark Parrish, Charles Toledo, John Mitchell, Darrin Gibson, Richard Blake, Trenor Wilkins, and Didier Barjon. I even took advantage of gathering information as simple as shoe details from Tampa's Running Center, training tips from Lee Stephens, and advice from the "Morris Bridge Sunday Training Group," and I wrote everything down.

Aside from running, I am also indebted to some of my mentors at Tampa Jesuit High School, who have helped develop: my writing skills (Mr. Kijanski, Ms. Brennan, Mr. Johnson, Mr. Charette, and Mrs. Charette); my artistic talents (Mrs. Mullen and Mr. Ball); and my character (Mrs. Batik, Mr. Suszynski, Mr. Mann, Mr. Sabin, Fr. Hermes, and Fr. Doyle).

Clearly, I am an easily coachable individual. I listen to coaches, and then act accordingly. I base my actions on several opinions and then take note of what works for me and what doesn't work for me. In order to write this book, I needed to be organized for ALL 4 years of my high school career, tracking several aspects of my running that may have seemed insignificant at first, but made all the difference in the long run: weight, shoes (size, date purchased, mileage), amount of time stretching, cross training methods and duration, how I felt after every run, eating habits, mileage (daily, weekly, and seasonal), and timing every run.

As a freshman, I was a mid-18:00 5Ker, who, as the #10 runner on my team, didn't even get to run at the 2A State Finals because my team was so competitive. Nonetheless, if I did have the opportunity to run, I still wouldn't have ranked in the top 100 runners in 2A. However, by the time I finished my senior year, I was easily ranked in the highest tier of all distance runners in Florida, and had earned: one state championship, 2 individual state runner-up titles, and 2 team state runner-up titles in cross country and track.

There were dozens of freshmen runners throughout Florida, and hundreds throughout the nation, that were at my level as freshman. So, what happened to those by the time we were all seniors? Well, a handful improved but far fewer got to the elite level. Some got injured, some got worse, and some quit running altogether. The point is simple – almost all of them needed some help and ALL of them could have benefited from this book.

The point of this book is not to see how superstars could get better, but rather how ordinary freshmen runners, like me, could turn into extraordinary seniors and beyond. This book chronicles my improvement in cross country and track during my high school career. Although I didn't make the varsity squad of my high school team as a freshman, through persistence, dedication, and a passion for running, I eventually was able to prove myself as one of the nation's finest high school distance runners.

Spoiler Alert
My Progression to
Where I Am Now

Hello, my name is Jordan Schilit. I have just completed my senior year at Jesuit High School (JHS) in Tampa, Florida and would like to tell you my story. I hope that writing this book will be an inspiration to all high school runners. Most runners never know how good they could be – you just have to have a method to the madness of distance running.

Every high school runner wants to get faster. Lucky for you, this book is a first-hand account of what goes through a high school runner's body and mind in the constant quest for improvement. Certainly, if there actually is a way in which you could improve your running, it only seems logical to keep reading and find out…

Where I Stand (or Run) Now

Ok, let me give you a few stats. Here are my personal records (PRs) as of my final race in high school:

- **5000m – 15:33** (that was indoors, which is equivalent to sub-15:20 on an outdoor track)
- **3200m – 9:22** (perhaps I could have gone faster that day, since I was 15 seconds ahead of the 2nd place runner)
- **1600m – 4:22** (I've raced the 1600m off and on for a couple of years and I am still learning how to race it; what's

impressive is that this race was tactical, with my last 800m in 2:02 and my last 400m in 0:58)

- **800m – 1:58** (my newest race; I just began racing it less than two months ago, so there's plenty of room for improvement here)

On top of that, despite not even making my high school Varsity team as a freshman, I finished my high school career with: one state championship medal, 2 individual state runner-up medals, and 2 team state runner-up trophies (all earned during my senior year) in cross country and track.

To put my performance in the proper perspective, there are approximately 100 high school distance runners in the country who have faster PRs than me (although anything can happen in any given race, since almost every one of us runs the 3200m in the 9:00-9:25 range). So, that means that I would not be the #1 recruit of any of the top collegiate running programs, but I'm good enough where most of the quality Division I programs would have an interest in me.

So, I'm not the fastest high school kid in the country. Therefore, most high school runners should be able to relate to me and should be able to accomplish everything that I have accomplished. I, like most high school runners, am a decent, yet not exceptional, athlete. It took lots of training, hard work, and discipline for me to achieve relatively speedy times.

3 Kinds of High School Runners

For simplicity, I have grouped all high school distance runners into the following 3 categories:

- Superstars
- Dormant superstars
- Everyone else

Here is how I would describe each of these categories:

- **Superstars** – These runners are immensely talented and often hard-working, typically achieving national prominence as a high school freshman. One of my mentors, Andy Biladeau, a JHS alumnus who graduated when I entered the school, was the #1-ranked freshman in the country as well as a national age-group record holder. As a freshman, he won the Gasparilla Distance Classic 5K in 15:45 as well as the Red Mule 5K in 15:03. Another superstar – my close friend and classmate, Connor Revord – was a national record holder in the 1500m and 3000m in middle school. Andy and Connor, aside from having great natural talent and great work ethics, were experienced runners before they came to Jesuit. Connor, in fact, came in 4th at the 1A State Finals in the 1600m while still in 8th grade. One more example for the guys is Berkeley Prep's Rolf Steier, who managed to win the 1A cross country individual State Championship for 4 years in high school; he continued his collegiate running career at Stanford University. On the girls' side, Floridians Kayla Hale and Ashley Brasovan both managed to win cross country individual State Championships for 4 years in 1A and 4A respectively. On the national scene, Jordan Hasay, who is perhaps the greatest girls high school distance runner to ever compete, not only managed to dominate California cross country for 4 years and win 2 Footlocker Nationals titles, but also qualified for the finals at the 2008 Olympic Trials in the 1500m. I, like more than 99% of the runners in this country could never come close to the talents of those superstars – especially not as a high school freshman. Perhaps, we can close the gap a little as sophomores, and a little more as juniors, and a little more as seniors – but it will take a lot of patience, discipline, and hard work to do that.

- **Dormant Superstars** – These runners have the talent, but are either new to the sport, haven't learned how to race, or are still getting the hang of developing a training regimen. For example, another one of my mentors – James "Ozzy" Osborne – was a senior at JHS during my freshman year. When Ozzy was a freshman, he was the 6th fastest runner in his grade and was a 19:30 5Ker. By his sophomore year, he was a low-16:00 5Ker. As a senior, he improved to the 15:30 level and won a State Championship in the 3200m during track season. Similarly, my good friends and training partners – Derek Wehunt (who was in my grade at nearby Sickles High School) and Mark Parrish (a year behind me at Chamberlain High School in Tampa) – were about my speed as freshmen. By their sophomore years, they both learned how to train and how to race, and eclipsed the 16:00 mark in the 5K. One example for girls in Florida is Brittany Koziara. Relatively unnoticed during both her freshman and sophomore years, she made dramatic time cuts as a junior and managed to qualify for Footlocker Nationals during cross country. On the track, she shocked a stacked 4A field to win the 1600m, beating current Stanford freshman Emilie Amaro and Duke-signee Ashley Brasovan. It's difficult mentally to compete against the dormant superstars because you may be beating them as a freshman but they are way ahead of you as a sophomore. Some of these dormant superstars make huge drops in one year and then continue to improve, although at a much lesser rate, in subsequent years. Other dormant superstars reach a plateau and simply never improve after their breakout years. For that reason, although it is sometimes frustrating for us to race against them, it's often more frustrating for them to race against us, since many of them have difficulty accepting the fact that they cannot make monstrous improvements year after year after year.

- **Everyone else** – The first two categories comprise a handful of great talents. There's not much that we can learn from them other than be patient, because hard-working, ordinary talents may someday catch up to superstars and dormant superstars. And, there's not much that I can teach them other than to be careful about doing 80 miles per week before your body matures, or you'll get injured. Yet for the more than 90% of runners – like you and I – who fall into the "everyone else" category, there are great opportunities to excel, if you're willing to work hard, work smart, set goals, and be patient. Although it took me four years to do so, it's amazing how many superstars and dormant superstars from my freshman and sophomore years wound up behind me by the end of my senior year.

Patience is essential. Over the past six years (from 7th through 12th grade), I have managed to improve significantly EACH year in EVERY distance that I have raced. In addition, I have improved at the SAME RATE for each of those years.

The Magic Formula

One of the most useful ways to track improvement is through the use of **VDOT** levels, a scale developed by running guru Jack Daniels, PhD (commonly known as "the world's best running coach" according to *Runner's World* magazine). Based on my performance, I have jumped exactly three VDOT levels every year, since I started running.

According to Daniels' Running Formula, a runner's VDOT is simply a measure of his/her current running ability. **Aerobic Fitness** is a measure of the efficiency of a runner's circulatory system, specifically the ability of your heart, arteries, and other blood vessels to continue delivering oxygen-rich blood to your working muscles. **VO$_2$max** is the maximum volume of oxygen your heart and lungs can deliver to your working muscles during fast running. VO$_2$max can be used to determine which workouts are suitable for the most effective improvement curve, whereas a VDOT (also referred to as the pseudoVO$_2$max) is strictly based on race performance.

Nonetheless, knowing your VDOT number on the Daniels' Running Formula chart, which is shown on the next two pages (Daniels, pgs. 48-49) is still an excellent indicator of how well you should be able to race.

Note: *Do not use the next table to see what your 5K racing pace for cross country should be, since courses vary significantly as a result of location, weather conditions, accuracy of course length, etc. Also, 5000m in the table means that the 5K distance would be raced on an outdoor track, which is typically faster than most certified cross country courses.*

Table 1   VDOT values associated with times raced over some popular distances

VDOT	1500	Mile	3000	2-mile	5000	10,000	15,000	1/2 Mara	Marathon	VDOT
30	8:30	9:11	17:56	19:19	30:40	63:46	98:14	2:21:04	4:49:17	30
32	8:02	8:41	16:59	18:18	29:05	60:26	93:07	2:13:49	4:34:59	32
34	7:37	8:14	16:09	17:24	27:39	57:26	88:30	2:07:16	4:22:03	34
36	7:14	7:49	15:23	16:34	26:22	54:44	84:20	2:01:19	4:10:19	36
38	6:54	7:27	14:41	15:49	25:12	52:17	80:33	1:55:55	3:59:35	38
40	6:35	7:07	14:03	15:08	24:08	50:03	77:06	1:50:59	3:49:45	40
42	6:19	6:49	13:28	14:31	23:09	48:01	73:56	1:46:27	3:40:43	42
44	6:03	6:32	12:55	13:56	22:15	46:09	71:02	1:42:17	3:32:23	44
45	5:56	6:25	12:40	13:40	21:50	45:16	69:40	1:40:20	3:28:26	45
46	5:49	6:17	12:26	13:25	21:25	44:25	68:22	1:38:27	3:24:39	46
47	5:42	6:10	12:12	13:10	21:02	43:36	67:06	1:36:38	3:21:00	47
48	5:36	6:03	11:58	12:55	20:39	42:50	65:53	1:34:53	3:17:29	48
49	5:30	5:56	11:45	12:41	20:18	42:04	64:44	1:33:12	3:14:06	49
50	5:24	5:50	11:33	12:28	19:57	41:21	63:36	1:31:35	3:10:49	50
51	5:18	5:44	11:21	12:15	19:36	40:39	62:31	1:30:02	3:07:39	51
52	5:13	5:38	11:09	12:02	19:17	39:59	61:29	1:28:31	3:04:36	52
53	5:07	5:32	10:58	11:50	18:58	39:20	60:28	1:27:04	3:01:39	53
54	5:02	5:27	10:47	11:39	18:40	38:42	59:30	1:25:40	2:58:47	54
55	4:57	5:21	10:37	11:28	18:22	38:06	58:33	1:24:18	2:56:01	55
56	4:53	5:16	10:27	11:17	18:05	37:31	57:39	1:23:00	2:53:20	56
57	4:48	5:11	10:17	11:06	17:49	36:57	56:46	1:21:43	2:50:45	57
58	4:44	5:06	10:08	10:56	17:33	36:24	55:55	1:20:30	2:48:14	58
59	4:39	5:02	9:58	10:46	17:17	35:52	55:06	1:19:18	2:45:47	59
60	4:35	4:57	9:50	10:37	17:03	35:22	54:18	1:18:09	2:43:25	60

VDOT	1500	Mile	3000	2-mile	5000	10,000	15,000	1/2 Mara	Marathon	VDOT
61	4:31	4:53	9:41	10:27	16:48	34:52	53:32	1:17:02	2:41:08	61
62	4:27	4:49	9:33	10:18	16:34	34:23	52:47	1:15:57	2:38:54	62
63	4:24	4:45	9:25	10:10	16:20	33:55	52:03	1:14:54	2:36:44	63
64	4:20	4:41	9:17	10:01	16:07	33:28	51:21	1:13:53	2:34:38	64
65	4:16	4:37	9:09	9:53	15:54	33:01	50:40	1:12:53	2:32:35	65
66	4:13	4:33	9:02	9:45	15:42	32:35	50:00	1:11:56	2:30:36	66
67	4:10	4:30	8:55	9:37	15:29	32:11	49:22	1:11:00	2:28:40	67
68	4:06	4:26	8:48	9:30	15:18	31:46	38:44	1:10:05	2:26:47	68
69	4:03	4:23	8:41	9:23	15:06	31:23	48:08	1:09:12	2:24:57	69
70	4:00	4:19	8:34	9:16	14:55	31:00	47:32	1:08:21	2:23:10	70
71	3:57	4:16	8:28	9:09	14:44	30:38	46:58	1:07:31	2:21:26	71
72	3:54	4:13	8:22	9:02	14:33	30:16	46:24	1:06:42	2:19:44	72
73	3:52	4:10	8:16	8:55	14:23	29:55	45:51	1:05:54	2:18:05	73
74	3:49	4:07	8:10	8:49	14:13	29:34	45:19	1:05:08	2:16:29	74
75	3:46	4:04	8:04	8:43	14:03	29:14	44:48	1:04:23	2:14:55	75
76	3:44	4:02	7:58	8:37	13:54	28:55	44:18	1:03:39	2:13:23	76
77	3:41+	3:58+	7:53	8:31	13:44	28:36	43:49	1:02:56	2:11:54	77
78	3:38.8	3:56.2	7:48	8:25	13:35	28:17	43:20	1:02:15	2:10:27	78
79	3:36.5	3:53.7	7:43	8:20	13:26	27:59	42:52	1:01:34	2:09:02	79
80	3:34.2	3:51.2	7:37.5	8:14.2	13:17.8	27:41.2	42:25	1:00:54	2:07:38	80
81	3:31.9	3:48.7	7:32.5	8:08.9	13:09.3	27:24	41:58	1:00:15	2:06:17	81
82	3:29.7	3:46.4	7:27.8	8:03.7	13:01.1	27:07	41:32	59:38	2:04:57	82
83	3:27.6	3:44.1	7:23.1	7:58.7	12:53.0	26:51	41:06	59:01	2:03:40	83
84	3:25.5	3:41.8	7:18.5	7:53.7	12:45.2	26:34	40:42	58:25	2:02:24	84
85	3:23.5	3:39.6	7:14.1	7:48.9	12:37.4	26:19	40:17	57:50	2:01:10	85

As Jack Daniels explains, "When you know your VDOT value, you can eliminate a great deal of guesswork from training and can avoid overtraining. I'll go so far as to say that your VDOT takes into account your psychological input into racing, because instead of using lab tests to determine your ability level, we're using your race performances, which are affected by your motivation and willingness to deal with discomfort. VDOT reflects everything that an individual calls on to perform in a race." (Daniels, pg. 46)

Daniels elaborates on the 'feeling' runners go through: "Intensity is of utmost importance; the intensity that you can maintain reflects the various reactions occurring inside your body, based on how long you're expected to be running in a race. Runners learn to deal with a certain level of discomfort for a certain period of time, regardless of how many miles they can cover in that time." (Daniels, pg. 47)

My VDOT Progression

In my case, this constant rate of progression of 3 VDOT levels each year since seventh grade has shown me the following:

- My body has gotten used to improving each year and will more than likely be comfortable in doing so in the future, as long as I continue my workout regimen
- I have steadily learned how to deal with more discomfort as I race each year, thus making me more competitive with racing
- I am a more competitive high school runner than I was a middle school runner
- Continuing this progression will only make me a more competitive college runner than I am a high school runner

Here is my VDOT level progression, along with my projected VDOT level progression, showing expected PRs and my actual PRs for the 1-mile and 2-mile:

VDOT Level	Year in school	VDOT Mile	Actual Mile	VDOT 2-Mile	Actual 2 Mile
54	7th Grade	5:27	5:28	11:39	11:40
57	8th Grade	5:11	5:10	11:06	11:10
60	9th Grade	4:57	5:00	10:37	10:39
63	10th Grade	4:45	4:46	10:10	9:57
66	11th Grade	4:33	N/A	9:45	9:45
69	12th Grade	4:23	4:22	9:23	9:22
71	College – Freshman	4:16	--	9:09	--
73	College – Sophomore	4:10	--	8:55	--
75	College – Junior	4:04	--	8:43	--
77	College – Senior	3:58	--	8:31	--

Note: *Even though I have improved 3 VDOT levels every year in high school, to be conservative, I have predicted improving 2 VDOT levels every year in college.*

The VDOT table is quite predictive. You develop racing experience as you mature in high school and you learn your true capabilities as you get older. Thus, the trend is as follows: the higher the VDOT, the more likely you are to be within a few seconds of <u>BOTH</u> the mile and 2-mile marks.

Over the past few years, I have gradually gotten bigger, stronger, and faster. Also, during that time period, I have gradually increased my base mileage, my average weekly mileage, and my workout intensity, and I have added cross training to my workouts. I've also left enough in the tank to enable me to continue to improve over my soon-to-start collegiate career at perennial Division III powerhouse Haverford College. So, unlike some of the high school superstars and dormant superstars who run 80 or more miles per week, my training regimen (which I'll describe in detail in Chapter 7) has progressed as follows:

- Middle School: averaged less than 10 miles per week of training throughout the year
- Freshman Year: averaged 30 miles per week of training throughout the year
- Sophomore Year: averaged 35-40 miles per week of training throughout the year
- Junior Year: averaged 45-50 miles per week of training throughout the year
- Senior Year: averaged 50-55 miles per week of training throughout the year

From Race Pace to Tempo Pace to Steady Pace to Easy Pace

Here is the progression of race PRs as well as racing ranges vs. my pacing for tempo, steady, and easy runs throughout high school. The basic trend is as follows:

- The **median race-pace** of my 5K racing range became my **tempo pace** for the following year
- The tempo pace became my **steady pace** for the following year
- The steady pace became my **easy pace** for the following year

This basic formula followed me through all four years of my high school career. Below is a visual representation of my racing paces as well as my training – i.e., tempo, steady, and easy – paces during the cross country seasons:

Year	5K PR	5K racing range	Median race pace	Tempo	Steady	Easy
9th	17:32	18:00 – 18:30	5:55	6:25	7:15	7:45
10th	16:55	17:20 – 17:40	5:40	5:55	6:25	7:15
11th	16:12	16:25 – 16:40	5:20	5:40	5:55	6:25
12th	15:44	15:50 – 16:05	5:06	5:20	5:40	5:55

(Training Paces)

Despite a few bumps along the road, I was extremely consistent throughout my performances each year of cross country. During my high school career, thanks to hard work and smart training (along with cross training), I went from a:

- decent (i.e., typically a 18:15 5Ker) during my freshman year to
- a good (i.e., typically a 17:30 5Ker) during my sophomore year to
- a very good (i.e., typically a 16:30 5Ker) during my junior year to
- an excellent (i.e., typically a 15:55 5Ker) during my senior year.

THE TREND IS QUITE APPARENT: INCREASED MILEAGE AT FASTER TRAINING PACES, COUPLED WITH ADDED STRENGTH AND HIGH QUALITY CROSS TRAINING, LEADS TO BETTER RESULTS.

With Success Comes Recognition

Here is another visual representation of my steady improvement curve. Notice that the tables on the next two pages show how I started off with minimal recognition during freshman year (the only recognition was that I lettered in cross country and track and was a member of a great team), but then achieved many significant honors by the time I finished my senior cross country and track seasons.

Cross Country
(15:44 PR in the 5K)

Freshman Year	*Sophomore Year*	*Junior Year*	*Senior Year*
		Team Captain	Team Captain
Member, State Champion team			Member, State Runner-Up team
			All-State
	All-County (Honorable Mention)	All-County (1st team)	All-County (1st team)
			ESPN RISE magazine Florida All-Area selection
		15th place - State	7th place - State
	5th place - Regions	4th place - Regions	Regional Runner-Up
		District Runner-Up	District Champion
	#3 or #4 runner on JHS team in most meets	#2 runner on JHS team in every meet	#1 or #2 runner on JHS team in every meet
			Member of State Runner-Up All-Academic Team

Track

(15:33 PR in the indoor 5000m, 9:22 PR in the 3200m, 4:22 PR in the 1600m, 1:58 PR in the 800m)

Freshman Year	*Sophomore Year*	*Junior Year*	*Senior Year*
		Team Captain	Team Captain, MVP Award
Member, State Runner-Up Team			Member, State Runner-Up Team
		All State (1st Team) – 3200m	All-State (1st Team) - 4x800m, 1600m, 3200m
		All-County	All-County (1st Team)
			Top-10 Nationally Ranked 4x800m team, school record holder
			ESPN RISE magazine Florida All-Area selection
			16th Place Nationally - Nike Indoor Nationals (5000m)
		6th Place - State (3200m)	STATE CHAMPION (4x800m), STATE RUNNER-UP (1600m, 3200m)
		4th Place - Regions (3200m)	Regional Champion (3200m); Regional Runner-Up (1600m, 4x800m)
8th place – Districts (3200m)	6th place - Districts (3200)	3rd place - Districts (3200m)	District Champion (3200m, 4x800m); District Runner-Up (1600m)

We're Student Athletes

I should point out that, although the focus of this book is on my high school RUNNING career, I have spent the past four years as a high school STUDENT, earning accolades for my academic and leadership skills as well, specifically:

- Honor student (graduated Summa Cum Laude from JHS)
- President of National Honor Society
- Editor-in-Chief of 3 school publications
- Recipient of Schwarzkopf Leadership Award (sponsored by U.S. Military Academy), presented to 5 outstanding high school scholar-athlete-leaders throughout the West Coast of Florida
- JHS's representative as top scholar-athlete for the Wendy's National High School Heisman Scholarship
- Recipient of an all-expense paid trip to travel to Poland and Israel for the "March of the Living" in a regional essay contest about the relevance of Elie Wiesel's memoir <u>Night</u> to today's society
- Contributor to several nationally recognized running publications; freelance writer
- Winner of "Best of Show" and "Best Senior AP Portfolio" at JHS Art show

* * * * * * *

One of the key characteristics of distance runners is discipline. And, one of the key characteristics of discipline is the ability to keep meticulous notes, logs, and records. Since the start of my high school career, I have chronicled my daily routines and have charted my progress. These records have been instrumental in my goal setting and I am happy to share that information with you. I will also go through my emotions throughout each season in cross country and track and eventually end up where this chapter began – where I am today.

My Introduction
to Running
How It All Began

My First Racing Shoes: Flip Flops

When I was eight years old, I went to watch my mom race in a local 5K in Tampa, Florida. I looked around at all of these strange people with crazy-colored retro shoes, listening to CD and MP3 players as they drank water and Gatorade. A few were even dressed up in costumes, sporting their favorite Disney character or superhero. Some 500 runners squeezed into one side of the University of South Florida's (USF's) narrow streets and then a horn sounded – the stampede began.

I thought I would never have anything to do with this madness, but then I saw my mom coming into the stadium. She wasn't exactly running in a straight line as her head bobbed from obvious dizziness. I didn't want to just leave her there struggling to finish her race in such miserable circumstances on a hot Florida afternoon, so I took off beside her…flip flops and all.

This story didn't really become public until the Tampa Tribune published a short article about how I started running. So, although I technically started running when I was 8, I was only a recreational road racer at that time. I was one of those people who showed up to fun runs or local 5Ks on Saturday mornings to see if I could keep up with my parents or beat some old guy that was running 26 minutes for 5K. I started running with both my mom and dad, but my dad was willing (and able at the time) to go faster if I wanted to do so. Eventually it was just the two of us, before his knees gave out and he had to stop running with me altogether.

But I continued running on my own simply because I loved the sport, not because I wanted to go out there and beat people. I was an innocent middle school runner who had never heard of a training plan, but liked going out for easy runs occasionally and showed up to Saturday road races to have a fun experience with my family.

Thankfully, my parents never pushed me. I picked up this sport on my own. I always thought it was wrong when parents try to live their childhood dreams through their children; it would never be about the kid in those situations, but rather about unrealistic goals set by parents.

My Middle School Years

Anyway, I continued running at the Hillel School of Tampa and joined its first cross country team during the fall of 2002 when I was 12 years old. I continued my running throughout middle school and, looking back at my performance, I was simply a good middle school runner. When I ran recreational 5K road races, I was barely breaking 19:00. In track meets, I was typically a mid-5:00 guy in the 1600m and a mid-11:00 guy in the 3200m.

I was talented enough at this point to be selected for the Junior Maccabiah team in Israel in the summer of 2005, but this selection was far less prestigious than for the Open division. For example, I only needed to run a 5:15 mile, whereas selection for the Open division required times under 4:20.

But I was still a little guy (as my pictures on the following pages will show) -- I was in the 70-75 lb range and less than 5 ft tall in middle school. I realized that winning local 5K age group divisions was nothing compared to high school State Championship races. I knew that I would be in for a major surprise during my freshman year of high school, yet, I still wanted to pursue this sport. There was just something about running around those soccer fields, on those tracks, and through those trails that gave me a sense of happiness.

I ran with my dad early on, hoping that he could help me place in my age group.

Running in my first race at the Hillel School of Tampa

Running alongside future Jesuit teammate Carson Holton

Standing next to future Jesuit teammate Sam Blouin. We had some great races in middle school and helped each other improve in both middle school and high school.

A cross country race in middle school, with my classic 2 feet off the ground pose

Competing in the Gasparilla Distance Classic 5K road race before starting my high school career – with my feet off the ground

Racing the 1500m at the 2005 Maccabiah Games in Israel

Standing with my brother, Bradley, after I competed at the Maccabiah Games in Israel

Freshman Year
VDOT 60

> Incoming Weight: 80 lbs.
> Outgoing Weight: 98 lbs.

Cross Country 2005

> Maximum Mileage: 38
> Average Mileage: 30

Introduction

Unlike in middle school, freshman year at Tampa Jesuit High School would be my first step towards an organized training regimen, where I learned the significance of running more quality miles in order to race faster.

My introduction to high school running was when our legendary coach, Mike Boza, invited five freshmen, including me, to travel to North Carolina for the cross country team's one-week summer training camp at Appalachian State University. During the summer months, we establish a strong base of mileage in order to maintain aerobic fitness throughout the season.

Not only was it difficult for me to run the distances of the talented and experienced upperclassmen from Jesuit, but I was humbled by my first taste of hill training. Either way, I knew I would have to get out of my comfort zone from middle school in order to reach a competitive level in high school.

Coach Boza taught me much more than just running, for example: how to improve my diet. Some kids may have eating problems in that they eat too much fast food or candy, but I was the complete opposite. In middle school, I stayed away from anything that wasn't a fruit or vegetable or pure protein, and was even nicknamed "rabbit" by my Maccabiah Team coach Todd Wolin. This strict diet may make sense for older people, especially for those who don't exercise on a regular basis, but Coach Boza stated the facts: I needed to grow. It was clear that I would need to build my body in order to compete with the bigger high school runners. So, I began eating from all the food groups. Coach Boza told me that: I needed to stop wiping the grease off of my pizza; and I must eat a dessert everyday, preferably ice cream, which was a source of calcium. The result was that I got steadily stronger during my freshman year, going from 80 pounds to nearly 100 pounds.

Training Program

For the first time in my life, I began a formal training program, beginning with my summer base training and eventually peaking at over 30 miles per week of training. Below is a basic overview of my daily freshman year cross country training. (I will provide greater detail of my training program in Chapter 7).

(Training Paces)

Year	5K PR	5K racing range	Median race pace	Tempo	Steady	Easy
9th	17:32	18:00 – 18:30	5:55	6:25	7:15	7:45

- **Easy:** 4-5 miles either continuous or with a few breaks. Once a week "long runs" of 6-8 miles during the summer base period. Typical pace of 7:30-8:30 per mile.

- **Steady**: Same distances as easy. Either:
  - o start off easy and get progressively faster (i.e. 8:15 pace per mile, then work down to 7:00 per mile); or
  - o a few miles to warm-up, then about 3 miles steady at approximately 7:00 pace per mile, then 1-2 miles to cool-down.
- **Tempo:** Shorter distances than easy or steady, but: 1 mile warm-up, then 2-3 miles at 6:15-6:30 pace per mile, then a cool down of a mile or less.
- **Interval:** These were the speed workouts, and took on a few different forms, as is illustrated below. During freshman year, the focus was primarily on split times for each repetition; eventually, I would learn to run the splits with minimal resting time (i.e., recovery) in between the splits. Here are some sample interval workouts during my freshman cross country season:
  - o "Pyramid of Power" (or "ladder workout") – with 2+ minutes of rest in between each rep and a 2-4 minute break midway through the entire workout (total workout of 3000m):
    - 200m in 0:35
    - 300m in 0:53
    - 400m in 1:11
    - 600m in 1:45
    - 600m in 1:45
    - 400m in 1:10
    - 300m in 0:52
    - 200m in 0:34
  - o 800m Repeats – with 2-3 minutes recovery in between each rep (total workout of 3200m):
    - 4x800m in 2:42, then 2:40, then 2:39, then 2:37
  - o 400m Repeats – with 2:30 recovery in between each rep; 5 minute additional break after 4 reps; another 5 minute rest after 6 reps (total workout of 3200m):
    - 4x400m in 1:08, then 1:10, then 1:12, then 1:12
    - 2x400m in 1:11, then 1:12
    - 2x400m in 1:11, then 1:10

Not Quite Good Enough

Jesuit High School (JHS) had won a cross country State Championship in 2004, and was the clear favorite to repeat as champs during my freshman season – 2005. That 2004 team of mostly juniors returned as seniors this year to dominate the pecking order among Jesuit runners, and now wanted to prove themselves as the best Jesuit cross country teams that we have ever had. As a 4'11" 80 lb incoming freshman, I was in awe of those guys. And, despite the fact that they were the greatest group of guys to be around and went out of their way to welcome me, I was intimidated by their sheer presence. That's where mind games begin, and it established a poor mindset for the rest of the season.

Ignoring my true talents and getting in the mindset that "I thought I wasn't fast enough," my goal was to be in the top-9 of the Jesuit team. In other words, I wanted to be the second-alternate of the 2005 cross country team.

What I did not realize at the time is when you set your goals too low, the expectations you set for yourself become even lower, and the result is that improvement is minimal. Although my times were good enough to be a top-7 runner on most teams, I wound up as the 10th runner on the Jesuit team that year, just missing the second alternate spot on a team that would eventually win the State Championship.

Here was the scenario: The top-7 was already set, so Coach Boza arranged for the next few guys hoping for alternate spots to have a run-off on the same day and on the same course as the 2A District 5 Championships. The result: I choked. I ran 17:57 on a fast course at Al Lopez Park. The longer version of this story is that I was so mentally weak with my running that I settled for decent – not excellent – times. Believe me, this was not laziness; I simply didn't know how to push myself to the next level. I wanted to get to that next level, but I just didn't understand yet what it took to do so.

Coach Boza and I agreed that although I may have been considered a decent runner, I was far from being an accomplished racer. One main aspect that I had yet to learn was that racing requires a distance runner to adapt to his/her situation. In other words, races do not always go as planned, and a runner must deal with how to avoid roadblocks along they way.

When I review my freshman season, I came to the realization that even though I raced in middle school, I was surely not ready for such a competitive field in high school (even if almost all of my races were against JV runners). Instead of being one of the fastest kids in the "Florida West Coast League" in middle school (which only consisted of 8 local schools), I was overwhelmed by the amount of competition that existed in high school running. Furthermore, I had not yet reached a very competitive mindset yet, so I was "running through quicksand."

Just an Unknown

Let's re-cap the season. The first race of my high school career was when Coach Boza allowed me and a few other freshmen to race in a 2-mile time trial, while all of the other freshmen raced a 1-mile time trial. After all of my summer base training and having gotten the opportunity to run with several runners of greater talent than myself, I only managed to run 11:20 for 2-miles. That night I blamed it on citric acid in my stomach from orange juice and some fast food I had eaten during the day, but looking back at the horrendous experience – I blew it. I was letting people beat me that I knew I was faster than. I was 14th on the team that night, and barely beat a couple of other underclassmen that probably would have passed me if the race was a few yards longer.

Probably the only successful and fast 5K race that I put together the entire season was my PR at the Red Mule Labor Day Race on August 27th, 2005. I managed to dip under the 18:00-barrier significantly, but on that short, fast course my 17:32 effort may not have been as impressive as I had once thought. More important was my place on the team – I was Jesuit's 8th finisher.

My near-miss from the top-7 squad landed me top-honors in the JV race in the following week's USF Invitational. I definitely let the heat get to my head during this race, and didn't even break 18:00. I had beaten Jesuit senior John Evans by 3 seconds at the previous week's Red Mule race, but he completely outraced me this week, running away with the JV victory in 17:26.

The next week I traveled to the FSU Invitational in Tallahassee, where the hills were much bigger and the course was more challenging. My time here was the slowest of the season – 18:34, and was not even good enough to place first on my team in the JV race. I could tell that I was under-trained for hilly courses and was unable to turn my legs fast enough when I needed to change my racing strategy throughout the race.

My 5K time improved slightly at the West Hillsborough Invitational Championships at the fast Al Lopez Park course in Tampa. However, that 18:11 on September 22nd simply was not sufficient. Not only did I fail to make the top-10 of the JV race, but I finished an abysmal 7th among Jesuit's JV (i.e., non top-7) racers. There was a pack of JHS guys from 17:32-17:37, but I didn't have the mental ability to say to myself, "They really are not running much faster than I am. I should be able to stay up with that crowd." Nonetheless, I fell off that group and the stragglers behind them, falling to 14th place overall in the JV race.

October 7th, 2005, at the very difficult Little Everglades Steeplechase Course, was a bit of a relief and a pleasant surprise, based on my prior race performances during this season. Although I did not break 18:00 once again, my 18:07 on this slow course on a very hot day was actually the 6th-fastest out of all Jesuit (Varsity and JV) runners that day. Perhaps I let that race give me too much confidence, since my next race (Bay Cup at Ed Radice Field in Tampa) was a disappointing 18:28 – and that was on a fast course.

However, I did manage to put in what I would call a "solid" race performance near the end of my freshman season at a 2-mile postal. Under the lights of JHS' track and during halftime of our 2005 homecoming football game, I raced to a PR of 10:51. Beating the #2 runner from Bishop Kenny (the catholic school we ran against that evening), I was the 7th place runner for Jesuit, although two of Jesuit's leading runners (Phil Scrivner and Mike Akins) had to drop out due to injury. Either way, I thought that I had secured my spot as the 2nd-alternate on the team, even though I certainly didn't have the mental toughness to seal the deal.

So, that brings us back to my initial scenario: I was considered to be the 9th fastest runner on the team, but failed to get the #9 spot on the team, simply because my goal was to be nothing higher than 9th place. Yet, I didn't have the confidence to race up with guys that were faster than me. I was weak, and I'll say it again – I choked.

Up until the State Championship, I wanted to get a gold medal so badly, and even more so, a State Championship ring. But I didn't deserve it; I truly hadn't learned how to race yet. Yes, the team won its title as "Repeat Champs," but it would have only been a pseudo-championship for me if I was simply given a state medal or a state ring. I had dreamed of standing next to the podium, but on that November 12th morning in Dade City, I finally realized that I would have to go get my own hardware. I wanted to earn all of these cross country memorabilia in the future, and I could only imagine the road that was yet to come.

Freshman Year Cross Country (5K) Results (2005):

Date	Race Name	Venue	5K Result
08/27/05	Red Mule 5K	McKethan Lake	**17:32**
09/09/05	USF Invitational (JV)	Idlewild Church	18:04
09/17/05	FSU Invitational (JV)	Miccosukee Greenway	18:34
09/22/05	West Hillsborough Invitational	Al Lopez	18:11
10/01/05	Flrunners.com Invitational (JV)	Little Everglades	18:07
10/11/05	Gasparilla Bay Cup	Ed Radice	18:28
10/25/05	District Championship (JV)	Al Lopez	17:57
11/26/05	Footlocker South Regional	McAlpine Greenway (NC)	18:19

In addition, I raced two 2-mile races on the track during Cross Country Season.

Date	Race Name	2-mile Result
08/16/05	2-mile Time Trial	11:20
10/07/05	Postal vs. Bishop Kenny	**10:51**

* * * * * * *

In summary, during my freshman cross country season, I was consistently an 18:15 runner, who was a bit faster on faster courses and a bit slower on slower courses. On a positive note, I did improve a little from my 18:30-19:00 road race times in the 5K from middle school. I was decent, but certainly not a star yet.

Track 2006

Maximum Mileage: 38
Average Mileage: 30

Introduction

After running through one season of high school training, I knew that track would be challenging, since I was definitely more of a cross country guy, who did better at longer distances, at this point. I even remember my dad saying to me then that I looked like I was just "going for a jog;" it didn't matter what distance I raced.

Training Program

Track season consisted of base #2, as Coach Boza called it, but the mileage was not as significant as cross country. In addition, speed workouts would start much earlier, since I was hoping to peak earlier in the season since I was not expected to be representing my team at the 2A State Track Finals, because we had several other more talented distance runners.

Here is how my training for my freshman track season differed from the cross country season that I had just completed (with details of my training sessions provided in Chapter 7):

- **Easy:** Same distances, but less amount of long runs.
- **Steady**: Slightly faster paces, but same distances.
- **Tempo:** Was more prevalent during track workouts. Faster training and more focused on intervals.
- **Interval:** Slightly faster paces. Recovery times and distances were essentially the same.

Nothing to Write Home About

With the cross country season behind us, it was now time to concentrate on track. The distance runners for Jesuit were surely among the best in Florida this year, and we all looked forward to an exciting season.

However, MY freshman year track season was very frustrating in that I did not have any fast leg speed: I couldn't kick when I needed to and I was constantly getting gapped by mediocre runners. I was much more in for a surprise during my freshman track season (where the races are 1600m and 3200m, as compared to the 5K in cross country) than I was for cross country because this different type of running emphasized a skill that I had not yet demonstrated – speed.

At the end of February of 2006, Coach Boza scheduled a time trial meet against Berkeley Prep in an attempt to give several runners a chance to run a PR in the 1600m, and for me, a chance at breaking 5:00. I failed to do so. I complained about my back hurting that day and was devastated by the number of runners on my team that beat me. Several Berkeley Prep runners also managed to convincingly break the 5:00 barrier, outdistancing me with my sluggish 5:08.

A couple of weeks later (March 4th) I got another shot to go under 5 minutes at the Nash Higgins Relay. Although this "cow heat" mile was jam-packed with bodies and the race was mid-day, there were still underclassmen in this race that ran under that nagging barrier. Once again, I failed to achieve that goal. It was my fault for not trying to stay with them after the first ½ mile: I was beaten by another freshman on my team and by a junior from Leto. I was just as fast as them, but of course my mind wasn't in it that day and was filled with doubt.

The Jesuit JV squad traveled back to Leto High School the following week for a small dual-meet. I raced the 2-mile, and ran to a slight PR of 10:45 – a 6 second improvement from my Postal during cross country season. I was happy to achieve the track letter standard (sub-11:00), but my goal was still to get the 5:00 mile standard as well. Unfortunately, my next race was more of the opposite, as I ran a 5:05 mile at the Chamberlain High School meet and fell out of the top-5 of Jesuit's JV milers.

The highlights of my track season were surely the two races that followed. On April 1st I ran a new PR of 10:39 for 3200m at the University of Tampa (UT) Distance Carnival, and only three days later, I ran 5:00.02 for the mile. True, I just missed breaking the 5:00 MILE mark, but my 1600m time equated to 4:58.28.

Unfortunately, however, I ended my season on a relatively low note at the 2A District 9 Championship. I placed 8th and scored 1 point for my team, but my time of 10:51 for 3200m was slower than my PR from several months ago. I was far off from advancing to Regions and it would have been nice to lower my time once again, but, if it's any consolation, I was one of only a handful of freshmen to break both 11:00 in the 3200m and 5:00 in the 1600m during the season.

State Championship... Without Me

I drove to Jacksonville with my dad to watch the 2006 track State Championship and got to watch some of the standout seniors on Jesuit's team place highly in many events. Several races were worth noting: the school record-holding 4x800m relay team cruised to a 1st place finish in 7:54.56 (a ten second gap over 2nd place), senior James "Ozzy" Osborne took 2nd in the 1600m (4:22) and 1st in the 3200m (9:28), freshman Connor Revord took 3rd in the 1600m (4:24, just 3 seconds off his PR), and junior Hunter Clausen placed 1st in the 400m with a new school record of 47.54.

With those scorers and other point contributors in the 800m, 4x400m, pole vault, and shot put, Jesuit racked up 60 points. This typically would be strong enough to win the State Championship by a landslide, but Godby High accumulated an unheard of 70 points. Jesuit took State Runner-up honors as a team, but, although I was on the team, I didn't receive – and certainly didn't deserve to receive – one of those silver medals. I knew that I would have the opportunity to run at the track Championship Finals some day and win several medals of my own.

Freshman Year Track Results (2006):

Date	Race Name	½ mile	mile	2-mile
02/21/06	Berkeley Dual-Meet	2:23	5:08	
03/04/06	Nash Higgins Relays		5:03	
03/08/06	Leto Dual-Meet			10:45
03/28/06	Chamberlain Dual Meet	**2:20**	5:06	
04/01/06	UT Distance Carnival			**10:39**
04/04/2006	Jesuit Home Meet		**5:00**	
04/11/2006	District Championship			10:51

In addition, I raced a 5K on the road after the track season ended.

Date	Race Name	5K Result
05/06/06	May Day 5K	18:09

* * * * * * *

In summary, freshman track season was pretty good for me. I improved about 10 seconds on my mile time and about 30 seconds on my 2-mile time from middle school. That is a 3-level VDOT improvement in one year, which is quite significant. In short, although I was pleased with my overall improvement, by the end of my freshman year, I was a decent track runner, but hardly a star, having failed to break 5:00 in the mile.

An art piece from my senior year that tried to capture my emotions from not being a part of the State Championship varsity squad

The 5 select freshmen (from left to right: me, Connor Rivard, Tatro, Joe Pa, and Connor Revord) that Coach Boza allowed to run in the 2-mile time trial in 2005. They all towered over me when we were in the 9th Grade.

Standing with Coach Boza after Jesuit's cross country banquet

Although I missed the 2nd alternate spot on the state championship cross country team, I still had my classic running pose and my ever-present shades.

Accomplishing the letter standard for the mile during my freshman year, while gliding through the air

Sophomore Year
VDOT 63

Incoming Weight: 105 lbs.
Outgoing Weight: 116 lbs.

Cross Country 2006

Maximum Mileage: 43
Average Mileage: 34

Introduction

No longer would seniors joke around with me about being that new little freshman. Even though I was still pretty small, I had "bulked up" to over 100 pounds, from my incoming freshman weight of 80 pounds. More important, I had enormous responsibilities this year; as a scorer for almost every varsity race, my performance would not only reflect my results, but rather those of the entire team. After every year that Coach Boza won a State Championship, he always made note that the key to Jesuit's victory was from the strength of the #5 guy (the final scorer).

Because of my importance to the team during races this year, Coach Boza emphasized to me my importance to stay with the varsity pack during every workout. He assured me that in distance running, one's training would always reflect how one races. More importantly, how one trains on days that one has to be mentally tougher is how one will perform on days when willpower is needed the most.

Training Program

Our summer base training once again began with our week-long annual trip to Appalachian State., where we could do some quality workouts on a hilly terrain. Once back in Tampa, here is how my training for my sophomore cross country season differed from my freshman cross country season (with details of my training sessions provided in Chapter 7):

					(Training Paces)	
Year	*5K PR*	*5K racing range*	*Median race pace*	*Tempo*	*Steady*	*Easy*
9th	17:32	18:00 – 18:30	5:55	6:25	7:15	7:45
10th	16:55	17:20 – 17:40	5:40	5:55	6:25	7:15

- **Easy:** Distances increased to 6-7 miles, with slightly longer long runs. Pace dropped to the low-7:00 range.
- **Steady:** Distances of 3-4 miles of steady running, with pace improving to 6:25 average per mile.
- **Tempo:** Same distance as prior year, but slightly faster pace (5:50-6:05 per mile).
- **Interval:** Still focused on split times, but recovery times shortened slightly. More mixing of different distances within workouts, as opposed to repeating the same distances.

Champions Run In Packs

Ready or not, it was time for the cross country team to re-prove itself worthy among Florida's best teams. Most people expected Jesuit to be a non-factor at this year's State Championship, since Connor Revord and Matt Hindman were the only returning athletes from last year's top-7. One weakness of the 2006 Jesuit team was something the 2005 team surely thrived on – pack running.

The seniors from 2005 and prior years had been taught by Coach Boza to run as one unit and to lay it on the line for their teammates – that's how to win championships. 2005's top-7 may have accomplished this well, but the class of 2000 still holds the record for tightest top-7 pack in Jesuit history (and perhaps in U.S. high school cross country history). The 2000 class won the State Championship with a 6 second spread from 1-7, and with the best runner on that team (Colin Strickland) finishing only in 21st place overall.

Keep in mind that most of Jesuit's successful cross country teams in past years were led by a strong group of seniors. We were fighting an uphill battle in this case, since our talented, but inexperienced, group of sophomores (the majority of our Varsity "A" and Varsity "B") squads would have to emerge as leaders. Even the two senior captains were hesitant to rely on our class at the time, but the reality of the situation was clear: our class would now be the backbone of this cross country team.

A Weight on My Shoulders

My first race of the season didn't get me off to a good start. I raced 10:49 for 2-miles in our traditional time trial at the beginning of the season, but I failed to come in at #2 for the sophomore class. I did not PR and was a bit distraught with some of my fellow classmates beating me after all of my summer training.

I did seem to redeem myself the following week at the Red Mule 5k. The course was measured accurately this year, so I was proud of my new PR (17:00) and for placing 3rd on Jesuit's varsity team. I beat our two seniors, although I did not make the top-10 individuals overall in that race.

The following week, I regressed to 4th place on the varsity team with my terribly slow time of 18:20. This course was extremely slow because of the rugged surfaces and numerous switchbacks throughout the Land O' Lakes High School course; the leaders (who were all consistent low-16:00 runners) struggled to break 16:50. Nonetheless, I was upset that I didn't improve my place on the team from the prior week's performance.

It was at this time that Coach Boza decided, since our pack-running strategy had failed thus far, that the varsity runners should race in smaller groups. The plan was that our #1 runner Connor Revord would, of course, be out in front, but Matt Tucker, Eric Bracy, Matt Hindman, and I would all try to stay together. The final two runners (which fluctuated between Connor Rivard, Alex Tatro, Logan Trimble, and Tony Giampa) would try to hang onto the tail end in a separate group. (Although it gets confusing, Connor Revord and Connor Rivard are two different runners on the Jesuit team; it was more confusing when Cade Rivard was also on our team.)

When we traveled to the University of Florida for the Mountain Dew Gator Invitational, I had mixed feelings about my end result. Although I ran a then-respectable 17:43 on UF's challenging golf course venue, I faded back into no man's land and, more disastrous, out of my group. Although I was our final scorer and managed to beat out a P.K. Yonge runner at the finish line, which enabled us to beat his team by a single point, I knew that I had failed my first true test. Racing on a hilly course like this should be a good indicator of how well I could perform at the challenging Little Everglades State Championship course, and failing on my coach's assignment did not help any argument that I could be trusted in a championship meet.

Becoming a Head Case

Then, the slump began. I worried so much about the UF meet that my race anxiety for the Flrunners.com Invitational escalated to such an extreme measure that I couldn't eat, sleep, or go for any type of relaxed running. I even missed a couple of days of school, simply from being too stressed to do anything other than feel sorry for myself. Despite having the opportunity to run on some very fast courses in cooler weather conditions, I had awful races during the next few weeks primarily due to stress. I failed to score for the team in all of those races, recording sub-par times – 17:58, 17:44, and 17:37 respectively – that frustrated me and my teammates.

I couldn't take it anymore; I wasn't getting better this season so far, and I couldn't get over the stress before every race. When I later talked to my dad about this issue his comment was, "You could do better. I can't explain myself clearer." I broke down in tears and couldn't believe his comment. I got angry with him because it seemed to me that he just didn't care about my racing any more. I thought he may have given up, since he may be tired of seeing me fail so often.

I didn't talk to him for about an hour and just sat in my room. I cried the entire time and questioned why I even started running, since it had made me into this mess – an unproductive boy who sat around and pondered his failures. After I finally had the courage to go back to talk to my dad, I told him bluntly, "I quit. I can't handle this anymore" and then ran off with the door shutting behind me.

My dad came in after a few minutes and said, "Look, Jordan, I didn't mean to offend you with my remark but your improvements from freshman year have been very subtle. Yes, you are getting a bit faster, but you should be crushing 17-minutes by this time. You're better than you give yourself credit. Stop getting mentally brought down by all of this and just move on." After going back and forth with him for several minutes, I stopped. I realized that this very arguing was what slowed me down; I was getting stressed over nothing. My dad had a point – I had been putting in so much energy into everything besides the actual race that I was completely worn-out by the time the race came.

For example, it seems perfectly reasonable for a student taking the SAT or ACT to be worn-out after 3-4 hours of standardized testing. In my situation, I was expending that much energy into useless thinking before my cross country races and by the time I had to perform, it translated into being tired mentally and physically.

So, it's true: I wanted to quit during the middle of my sophomore cross country season, simply because race anxiety was so overwhelming at that time. But after talking it through with my dad, he convinced me to give it another try – worry free. I realized that when I throw out the stress from racing and get into my own positive mindset, distance running truly is my passion.

Bouncing Back

It wasn't surprising that my next three races, which were stress-free, were all outstanding performances. On October 21st, I raced in a 3200m Postal at Hernando High School and recorded a PR by over 20 seconds – 10:20. The next week, we headed back to Al Lopez Park. Coach Boza, although assuring me that I would still get to run varsity at the State Championship, wanted me to run in the open race at Districts so that he could decide on the other four sophomores that were competing for three spots on our top-7. I knew that Coach Boza wanted to help me out in this case; he put me in a different race, but it was the same course as the 2A District 5 Championships – I just wouldn't have to worry about any other competition creeping into my head. It was my job in this race to simply run to my true potential. Sure enough, I broke 17:00 for the first time in my high school career and ran the 4th fastest time out of any Jesuit runner that day. And, I did it during the much hotter JV race, running the entire race 30 seconds ahead of the rest of the field.

The next race, despite 30 mph winds and a slow, swampy Ed Radice course, I managed a near-PR of 17:09, placing 5th overall at the Regional Championship. I truly had stepped it up, and I knew that I had performed at a sub-16:50 level that day and made my coach, my teammates, and my parents proud.

It was unfortunate the next week, at the State Championship, however, that the team as a whole truly let Coach Boza down. Belen Jesuit ran away with the title that year, and none of us were prepared to stay with them on the hills of Little Everglades.

This season had dragged, and I realized I would put the negatives behind me and learn from my new mental enlightenment of distance running, and get ready for the upcoming track season.

Sophomore Year Cross Country (5K) Results (2006):

Date	*Race Name*	*Venue*	*5K Result*
08/26/06	Red Mule 5K	McKethan Lake	17:00
09/09/06	Land O' Lakes Gator Invite	Land O' Lakes H.S.	18:20
09/16/06	UF Gator Invite	UF Golf Course	17:43
09/29/06	Flrunners.com Invitational	Ed Radice	17:58
10/07/06	FSU Invitational	Miccosukee Greenway	17:44
10/13/06	Gasparilla Bay Cup	Ed Radice	17:37
10/25/06	District Championship (JV)	Al Lopez	**16:55**
11/03/06	Regional Championship	Ed Radice	17:09
11/11/06	State Championship	Little Everglades	18:04
11/18/06	Footlocker South Regional	McAlpine Greenway (NC)	17:34

In addition, I raced two 3200m races on the track during cross country season

Date	*Race Name*	*3200m Result*
08/17/06	Time Trial at Jesuit HS	10:49
10/21/06	Postal at Hernando HS	**10:20**

* * * * * * *

This was an interesting cross country season with lots of lows and lots of highs. In terms of overall performance, I did improve this year from last year — I was consistently running in the 17:30 to 18:00 range as a sophomore, and even broke the elusive 17:00 barrier; by contrast, as a freshman, I rarely got below 18:00 in the 5K.

Although this was my worst – and most frustrating – season and certainly the low-point of my running career, I learned more this season than any other. I learned how to deal with adversity and bounce back through mental roadblocks to a strong finish. In that way, it was my most important season, since the lessons we learn in life come from our failures, not from our successes. And, boy, did I fail – so I certainly learned quite a bit.

This is the one season that gave me the mental toughness to show that I could deal with adversity. I was ready to quit racing, but instead had a:

- PR for 3200m in the Postal at Hernando High School
- PR for 5K at Districts; sub-17:00 shows you have enough talent for the elite level and puts you "on the radar". 16:55 is a whole lot better on a resume than 17:01. Also, I ran by myself on a hot day
- PR-EFFORT performance at Regions – 5th place, 17:09. 3rd on team.

I knew I was ready for the track season and by concentrating on the 3200m, I would be able to focus on my place in the State, rather than on my place on our team.

Track 2007

> **Maximum Mileage: 40**
> **Average Mileage: 32**

Introduction

Switching my focus once again to track training, I would be able to focus on my individual times, rather than on the team's overall performance, since our team was not strong enough to be in contention for a state title. After a disappointing 8th place finish at last year's District 3200m race, I was determined to make it to Regions, and possibly to the State Championship.

But, even if I were to advance in these races, I would not have the weight of the team on my shoulders. Therefore, there were time goals (i.e. sub-10:00 for the 3200m) that I felt were necessary to hit during this season.

Training Program

Here is how my training for my sophomore track season differed from my sophomore cross country season (with details of my training sessions provided in Chapter 7):

- **Easy:** Same distances and pacing as during cross country.
- **Steady**: Typically 4 miles of steady running, with same pacing as during cross country. Integration of striders afterwards to get in some extra turnover.
- **Tempo:** Either 3 miles continuous or 2 x 2mile tempos; same pace (5:50-6:05 per mile).
- **Interval:** More common than tempo runs; workouts started to exceed racing distances (i.e. more than 1600m or 3200m).

Coach Boza's Impact

After the cross country season ended, Coach Boza shocked us all when he called us into a meeting one afternoon to announce his resignation. He would be leaving to coach at Leto High School, hoping to re-build what Florida used to call "The Long Red Row." Leto used to be one of the powerhouses in Florida, similar to what Coach Boza, who was a Jesuit alumnus himself, created at Jesuit, but had fallen into a major slump in recent years.

When Coach Boza left after my sophomore year of cross country, I realized how much of an impact he would have on my life. Coach Boza was like a second father to me; he kept me under his wing and taught me everything there was to learn about running. Furthermore, he taught me that how you deal with problems in running would be how you would live your life as a man in the real world.

That year especially taught me the importance of well-qualified coaches. When I entered high school I was ready to bring my running to a whole different level, and of course thought that Coach Mike Boza would be of great help along the way. Coach Boza helped Jesuit to its first State Championship in 1998, and won three more titles: 2000, 2004, and 2005.

I had known Coach Boza before entering Jesuit High School. He used to joke that "he had known me since I was just a little guy…and I was still just a little guy" throughout the time that he had coached me. We were family friends and Coach Boza always had taken an interest in my running from when I was very young. He always had the faith in me that I would get to the elite level in high school and hopefully translate that success in later years to college running. As my head coach at Jesuit for my freshman and sophomore years, he gave me detailed schedules of workouts – marked out with daily, weekly, and monthly mileage. It was even more specific as to what workout we should be doing each day, the type of week we would be training for (races/no races, etc…), and the "seasonal mode" that we were in – i.e. base, tempo, interval, race, championship….

However, I felt the impact of Coach Boza's help after he left mostly because of the lack of his presence – he taught me to be independent in the same way that a good parent teaches his kids to get along on their own. I realized that when Coach Boza was no longer there to give us workout packets and cross country/track seasonal analyses. It was surely the time that made me think: "Maybe it's my turn to make these charts. I am going to have to be the one to collect all of this data if I truly want to maximize my talents."

Seemingly Smooth

After two sub-par performances in February, my running started clicking during a Jesuit tri-meet vs. Plant and Sickles. I slightly lowered my 3200m PR from the past cross country season with a 10:18. Coach Rodriguez, our head track coach, and I agreed that the 3200m would be my strongest event this season, and felt that I would have a legitimate shot at getting to the Regional Championship if I only ran that one event.

I did end up running two 1600m races this season in an attempt to work on my closing speed for longer distances. On March 10th, I ran a then-solid PR of 4:46 on a very hot, sunny afternoon. Probably more of an accomplishment was my 4:48

in the "cow heat" 1600m at the Bob Hayes Invitational, which had over 40 people racing against each other.

The definite highlight of my 2007 track season was surely under the lights at the UT Distance Carnival, where I had the luxury of being in a stacked race. I placed 9th with a 9:57 in a race which had 10 guys breaking 10:00 and several others under 10:20. I continued to run in the low-10:00 range for the next two weeks at the Wharton Dual-Meet and FSU Relays, running 10:08 and 10:07 respectively. I noticed that I could run these times simply because of my fitness now, not necessarily because of competition. I figured that I would be able to run in the low-10:00s or just under 10:00 at Districts and thus have a shot at advancing to Regions.

A Near Miss … for the Better

On April 12th, 2007 I competed in the 2A District 9 Championship at Berkeley High School. Somehow, perhaps because of the strength of the field, I got psyched out in this race and did not test my limits fully. I sat in the middle of the pack and failed to make a name for myself. Furthermore, I ran my slowest 3200m race in several weeks, dropping to 6th place with my 10:14 effort. I was well behind the 4th and final qualifying spot for Regions (10:05). That runner was Berekeley Prep freshman phenom Tyler Greathouse, who typically beat me in middle school as well.

Even though it would have been an outstanding accomplishment to advance to Regions (and possibly State Finals) as a sophomore, I still wasn't mentally prepared at that point to run with the state's best. If I had run that 10:05 time that I needed to extend my season by another week, perhaps I would have gained a false sense of confidence that I belonged with that top-4 group of runners. Realistically, one sub-10:00 performance during the season was not enough to prove that I could be a contender for scoring at the State Championship. Essentially, I needed some other race to prove that I could regain my confidence after failing the week before.

Bouncing Back, Again

Like I did during the cross country season in my sophomore year, I again learned how to deal with adversity. I had momentum going into the District Meet, but failed to qualify for Regions, and now I would need a way to bounce back from this roadblock in my career.

The week after my disappointing showing at Districts was when I realized how much "I needed to step up my game" if I wanted to get to that next level. I decided to prolong my season for a few more weeks and to compete in some local 5K road races. On April 20th, I competed in the Spartan Sprint 5K and recorded a new PR of 16:17. Even though the course was measured to be 150m short (so my true time was approximately 16:42), I knew that this race was not a fluke because I never raced over 17:00 again. A week later, I improved on my prior year's time of 18:09 at the GunAllen Financial May Classic in running a 16:33 on a USATF certified course.

Sophomore Year Track Results (2007):

Date	Race Name	1600m	3200m
02/24/07	Steak n' Shake Invitational		10:50
03/07/07	Tri-meet vs. Plant and Sickles		10:18
03/10/07	Charles Johnson Invitational	4:46	
03/17/07	Bob Hayes Invitational	4:48	
03/24/07	UT Distance Carnival		9:57
03/27/07	Wharton Dual-Meet		10:08
03/30/07	FSU Relays		10:07
04/12/07	District Championship		10:14

In addition, I competed in two 5K road races after the track season ended.

Date	*Race Name*	*5K Result*
04/20/07	Spartan Sprint 5K	16:17**
05/05/07	GunAllen Financial May Classic	**16:33**

** Note: *The Spartan Sprint 5k was re-measured afterwards to be 150m short, so my time would have been slower than the clock showed, but nonetheless would still have resulted in a significant PR (approximately 16:42).*

* * * * * * *

One could say that having run under 10:00 in one race, but not even qualifying for Regions, was overall a failed season. I would disagree, however, since this season was an excellent learning experience. Yes, my performance at Districts was a failure, but I managed to run new PRs (9:57 for 3200m and 16:33 for 5K) that made me start to focus on my overall ranking in Florida, rather than simply on my ranking on our team. I knew that I could maintain the #2 spot on Jesuit's team, and hopefully begin to be recognized as one of the elite runners in the state.

Overall, track season was a success, with another 3-level improvement on the VDOT scale. I was breaking 5:00 in the 1600m convincingly, with a 15 second improvement from freshman year, and consistently being in the 10:00-10:15 range for 3200m – and actually broke 10:00 one time this season, with a huge 40 second improvement from the prior year. Sub-10:00 is a good indicator of whether or not you could score at the State Championship meet. Also, track times are more reliable than cross country times, so this mark is very appealing to many college coaches.

In addition, my disappointing showing at Districts, where I ran one of my slowest times of the season (sub-par, choked under pressure), had a positive outcome. I used that failure to get me motivated for some 5K road-races where I firmly established myself as a sub-17:00 runner and capable of doing some great things during my upcoming junior year.

Still shorter than my entire class during my sophomore year

Finishing in 5th place at the Regional Championship my sophomore year

Competing at the Steak n' Shake Invitational

Junior Year
VDOT 66

Incoming Weight: 119 lbs.
Outgoing Weight: 125 lbs.

Cross Country 2007

Maximum Mileage: 59
Average Mileage: 40

Introduction

After hitting some significant marks during my sophomore track season, I hoped to transcend the Jesuit pack and to be known as an elite runner in Florida. Getting to that level allowed me to start training with my good friend and Jesuit classmate, Connor Revord, who was for the past few years a nationally recognized runner. Even though I was not able to stay up with him each workout, I knew that trying my hardest to stay up with him would help my race performances in the future. Also, the team was now under the wing of head coach Greg Maurin, who hoped to tweak our training regimen towards a more successful peak than last season, hopefully culminating in winning a team State Championship.

Training Program

After our week-long annual summer training at Appalachian State, we continued our summer and fall training in Tampa. Here is how my training for my junior cross country season differed from my sophomore cross country season (with details of my training sessions provided in Chapter 7):

(Training Paces)

Year	5K PR	5K racing range	Median race pace	Tempo	Steady	Easy
9th	17:32	18:00 – 18:30	5:55	6:25	7:15	7:45
10th	16:55	17:20 – 17:40	5:40	5:55	6:25	7:15
11th	16:12	16:25 – 16:40	5:20	5:40	5:55	6:25

- **Easy:** Distances increased to 7-8 miles, with long runs being more routine and also continuing until later in the season. Pace was now in the mid-6:00 range.
- **Steady**: Distances now 4 miles of steady running, with pace improving to sub-6:00 pace per mile.
- **Tempo:** Distances now the same as steady runs; no longer broken up; pace improved as well (5:40 pace per mile).
- **Interval:** Split times getting much faster; recovery times decreasing to under 1:00 between reps for shorter workouts, and no more than 2:00 between reps for longer workouts. Breaks midway through workouts were rare.

The "Other Guy"

During my junior year, I found myself as the clear #2 runner for Jesuit High School. Yet, forum talk usually consisted of: Connor Revord, "the other Jesuit guy" (i.e., me), and the Jesuit cross country team as a whole. However, people were slowly beginning to notice my consistent top-5 or top-10 finishes among fairly strong fields as the season progressed.

My first race of the season was much stronger than my time showed. At the Southern Stars Sunset 5K, I finished 5th behind runners that all had PRs under 15:50. Times ran about 40-50 seconds slower than PRs because of the wet, muddy, and sloppy fields, so I was very pleased with my 16:52 time there.

On September 1st, we returned to the fast course at the Red Mule 5K. I placed 2nd overall with a season-best of 16:24, even though this year's event was not as stacked as usual. However, I realized it was a good sign that I could convincingly break 16:30, running by myself.

Two weeks later, the Jesuit cross country team started its official racing season at the Land O' Lakes Gator Invitational. I definitely made a statement this week, placing 4th overall in a very competitive high school field and managing to beat last year's winning time. Even though my 5K time was only 16:39, it was over a 1:30 improvement from last year's effort, partially as a result of a strong kick at the finish. I finally learned how to finish races convincingly this year, but a 15 second surge would still not be enough to stay up with the elite finishers in the state.

A Different Mindset

During much of my freshman and sophomore years, I really did not enjoy racing. Although I was improving, I didn't see the results nearly as obvious as during my junior year cross country season. Most importantly, my mental mindset was much tougher during my junior year; thus, I wanted to go out and show my full potential. I didn't think that way during my first two years of high school. I was "psyched out" way too often once the pressure of races was put on my shoulders.

So, when the FSU Invitational approached, I wanted to prove myself as among the state's elite, since this race always showcased very strong talent. Unfortunately, I would be observing the Jewish High Holy Day, Yom Kippur, the day of that race, and was not able to compete at the FSU Invitational. Instead, I raced in a dual-meet against Plant High School in order to get some race experience. Although I raced all alone, I managed to run 16:29 – only a few seconds off my Red Mule time from earlier in the season.

Competition was definitely a factor the following week, when I ran to a new PR of 16:14 at the Southern Stars Invitational. Placing 13th overall in the 2nd-biggest race in Florida, I thought that my performance was very solid. However, I knew that once my kick developed into a bigger threat, I would be passing more people towards the end of these races and eventually dip below the 16-minute barrier.

Finally, Some Recognition

The day after I turned 17, I was recognized in the above piece (my first featured article) in the newspaper. True, this piece was not lengthy, but it was a sign of what would come in the future: more recognition for my consistent improvements.

Peaking in November...

After running 16:42 at the flrunners.com Invitational and 16:35 at the Hillsborough County Championship, I felt ready to turn in my best performances in November, during Districts, Regions, and most importantly, the State Championship. Even though I had run at the cross country State Championship last year as a sophomore, this was the first season where I really needed to peak for the State series. That year, my team and individual performances were vital. In addition, after running a PR of 9:45 for 3200m, trailing Sickles' star Derek Wehunt by only 8 seconds, I had plenty of momentum going into Districts.

A few days later, I ran to a new 5K PR of 16:12 at the 2A District 5 Championship, finishing in 2nd place, only 12 seconds behind 2-time District Champion Connor Revord. That was a 23 second improvement on this course from a few weeks ago.

The next week, we traveled to the Estero Community Park to race on a very slow, sandy, hilly, windy course at the Regional Championship. Almost all of the top-15 runners ran times 40 seconds slower than their PRs, so this race was purely about place. Although not quite as strong of a showing as the prior week, my 16:59 was good enough for 4th place.

...But a Near Miss

However, at the State Championship, we were in for a big surprise. Everyday over the following year, I had flashbacks of the announcer saying, "And that should seal the deal for Belen Jesuit..." The press called it Tampa Jesuit's "One Bad Day," since we were undefeated during the regular season, but came up short at the State Championship. Furthermore, Belen Jesuit completely caught us by surprise, since we had beaten them twice during the regular season.

This was a sub-par performance for me individually too. Although I had improved from the prior year's 18:04 to a 16:44, I still wanted to run a mid-16:00 or low-16:00 time. Any way you look at where my performance ranks among performances throughout the season, the point is simple – your last race of the season should be your best race of the season. In essence, I choked under the pressure, even if I did manage a respectable 15th place finish.

Nonetheless, the strength of my junior season was recognized by the St. Pete Times, which gave me a spot on the First Team All-County roster.

St. Petersburg Times
Published: November 22, 2007

All-Hillsborough County Boys Cross Country Team

Runner of the Year: Derek Wehunt, Jr., Sickles
Coach of the Year: Mike Boza, Plant

First Team

Connor Revord, Jesuit, Jr.: Top runner for county's top team; took fifth in 2A (16:11), only local to beat Wehunt head-to-head.

Mark Parrish, Chamberlain, So.: Finished fourth with the county's top time at state (15:58).

Drew Woodke, Brandon, Sr.: Capped off back-to-back district titles with 14th-place finish at state.

Duncan Hock, Plant, Sr.: Broke school record (16:10) in leading Panthers to fourth-place finish in 3A.

Richard Blake, Berkeley Prep, Sr.: Wrapped up third consecutive top-5 finish at A meet (16:17, third).

Keegan Bixler, Newsome, Jr.: Took 10th at state (16:10) but highlight was victory at Southern Stars.

Jordan Schilit, Jesuit, Jr.: Revord's right-hand man kept pace in low 16s, topping out at 16:14.

Some Unfinished Business

I knew that my senior year would be a battle once again for the State Championship, and hopefully with cooler weather, I wanted to lead my team to its first title since 2005. But before track even started, I wanted to run some road races in Tampa to prove that I could maintain paces in the low-16:00 range.

I was pleased with my first effort, where I ran 16:30 on a hilly course against mostly collegiate runners at the Turkey Trot 5K. Then, on a comparable course 2 weeks later, I lowered my time slightly with a 16:26 at the Bolt Run 5K. However, the highlight of my post-season road racing was at the Madd Dash for Sadd 5K, where I recorded a new PR of 16:04. This was a very fast course, and I took advantage of the opportunity to run just over 16:00. I would be looking forward to lowering my PR once again during my senior year, with the hope of going under 16 minutes.

Junior Year Cross Country (5K) Results (2007):

Date	Race Name	Venue	5K Result
08/24/07	Southern Stars Sunset 5K	Ed Radice	16:52
09/01/07	Red Mule 5K	McKethan Lake	16:24
09/15/07	Land O' Lakes Gator Invitational	Land O' Lakes High School	16:39
09/19/07	Plant Invitational	Al Lopez	16:29
09/29/07	Southern Stars Invitational	Ed Radice	16:14
10/06/07	Flrunners.com Invitational	Chain Of Lakes Park	16:42
10/18/07	Hills. County Championship	Lake Park	16:35
11/01/07	District Championship	Lake Park	**16:12**
11/09/07	Regional Championship	Estero Comm. Park	16:59
11/17/07	State Championship	Little Everglades	16:44

In addition, I competed in three road races after my final cross country race of my junior season.

Date	*Race Name*	*5K Result*
11/22/07	Turkey Trot 5K	16:30
12/01/07	Madd Dash for Sadd 5K	**16:04**
12/08/07	Bolt Run	16:26

Also, I raced in a 3200m Postal, which included the top runners from the following schools: Jesuit, Sickles, Robinson, Plant, and Brandon.

Date	*Race Name*	*3200m Result*
10/07/07	3200m Postal at UT	**9:45**

* * * * * * *

Things finally clicked during my junior year cross country season. I was clearly a 16:30 runner, or better, showing I could be one of the top runners in the state. I went through significant improvement, running nearly a minute faster on average from sophomore year, and bettering my PR by about 45 seconds.

Track 2008

Maximum Mileage: 54
Average Mileage: 36

Introduction

Following lots of momentum from a very strong cross country season, I hoped to have even a stronger track season during my junior year. However, the unthinkable happened – my season was shortened, and nearly wiped out, as a result of a stress fracture in my foot. That taught me to listen to my body; training harder is not always the wisest decision – a distance runner must learn from his mistakes and train as smartly as possible.

Training Program

Below is a basic overview of my junior year track workouts. However, I was very limited with RUNNING workouts due to my stress fracture. So, I needed to take advantage of cross training to stay in shape. Here is how my (limited) training for my junior track season differed from my junior cross country season, with details of the entire season shown in greater detail in Chapter 7:

- **Easy:** Distances increased to 7-8 miles, with long runs being more routine and also continuing until later in the season. Pace was now in the mid-6:00 range.
- **Steady:** Distances now 4 miles of steady running, with pace improving to sub-6:00 pace per mile.
- **Tempo:** Distances now the same as steady runs; no longer broken up; pace improved as well (5:40 pace per mile).
- **Interval:** Split times getting much faster; recovery times decreasing to under 1:00 between reps for shorter workouts, and no more than 2:00 between reps for longer workouts. Breaks midway through workouts still occurred, but were rare.

Staying On Top Of My Game...
While Underwater

My junior year track season was a blessing in disguise. I now realize that building up too quickly and starting speed workouts too early in the season can only make you more vulnerable for a runner's worst nightmare – injury. After finding out that I had a hairline fracture of the third metatarsal bone of my right foot, I realized that there would have to be other ways for me to stay in shape other than running. The basis of my training was definitely swimming, where I was able to find a balance of both aerobic and anaerobic workouts. I tried to simulate all of the running workouts that I had planned to do this season (i.e. easy, steady, tempo, and interval training) in the water. Those workouts are also presented in Chapter 7.

Comeback of the Year

After missing 6 weeks of running due to a stress fracture, I nonetheless managed to break 10:00 in the 3200m at Districts, where I placed 3ʳᵈ. I lowered my season-best by a few seconds with my 9:56 effort the following week at Regions, which was good enough for 4ᵗʰ place. Not only did this allow me to run in the first FHSAA Track Finals of my high school career, but I would also have the opportunity to get some redemption from this year's cross country season. Even the press recognized my accomplishments:

The Tampa Tribune
Published: April 15, 2008

By: Bill Ward

COMEBACK OF THE YEAR? That might go to **Jesuit's Jordan Schilit.** He suffered a stress fracture in his foot early this season but managed to stay fit enough during the recovery period to advance out of Wednesday's Class 2A-District 9 meet with a third-place effort in the 3,200-meter run. Schilit's time (9:59.55) is the third best performance heading into Thursday's 2A-Region 3 meet in Titusville, meaning he has a good shot at reaching the state finals.

http://www2.tbo.com/content/2008/apr/15/sp-bulls-coaching-tradition-continues-with-littlet/sports

©2008 Media General Inc. All Rights Reserved.

I went into the State Championship race mentally prepared and wanted to stay with the leaders as long as possible. I went through the first mile in under 4:50, but faded from 3rd to 8th place during lap 5. I managed to pass two of those guys during the last 400m, finishing in 6th place at the 2008 State Championship. My time of 9:50.19 was only 5 seconds off my PR and my 3 points that I contributed help Tampa Jesuit place 8th in the team standings; as a consolation, we beat our longtime rival and defending State Champs Belen Jesuit by 3 points.

Junior Year Track Results (2008):

Note: *I missed the majority of the season due to a stress fracture (out 6 weeks), but still placed 6th at the State Championship, off of 4 weeks of running.*

Date	*Race Name*	*3200m*
04/09/2008	District Championship	9:59
04/17/2008	Regional Championship	9:56
04/26/2008	State Championship	9:50

* * * * * * *

Although I ran in only three races, I improved in EVERY race and was clearly in the 9:50 range, which was excellent considering I could not start running again until the week of Districts (I missed 6 weeks of running). Despite that, with my 9:45 PR during cross country season, I improved my usual 3 levels on the VDOT scale and went from a runner who could not break the 10:00 barrier to one who routinely ran sub-10:00, which is the indicator of getting into the elite category.

Posing with the five original freshman, (once again, from left to right: me, Connor Rivard, Tatro, Joe Pa, and Connor Revord), but during our junior year. We all "bulked up" quite a bit since our freshman picture. Other juniors who played a key role on our team were Logan Trimble, Ben Martin, and Mikey Gonzalez.

Sitting with Coach Boza after the Plant Dual Meet in Al Lopez

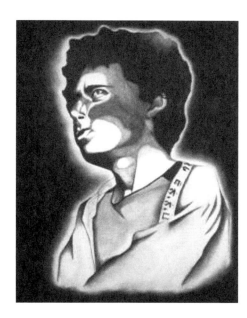

I made this art piece during my senior year, describing my devotion to Judaism; I chose not to run at the FSU Invite in 2007 because it conflicted with Yom Kippur

Celebrating our team victory at the 2007 Flrunners.com Invitational Race of Champions

Hanging with Lee Stephens through a swampy Ed Radice soccer field during the 2007 Sunset 5K

Kicking on the homestretch against Mark Parrish, edging out my training partner for 4th place

Placing 2nd at the 2A District 5 Championship as a junior, I ran a cross country PR of 16:12

Only my second week of running during my junior year track season, I broke 10:00 in the 3200m at districts.

Finishing my "Comeback of the Year" by placing 6th at the Class 2A FHSAA Track State Finals. Photo courtesy of *flrunners.com*

Waving to the crowd after the announcer made known my significant accomplishment

Senior Year
VDOT 69

Incoming Weight: 130 lbs.
Outgoing Weight: 137 lbs.

Cross Country 2008

Maximum Mileage: 66
Average Mileage: 47

Introduction

By this time, I made sure I was all healed and ready to go. I would be a clear leader on this team and I knew that I was one of the few that controlled the team's shot at a State Championship. I wanted to make sure that I ran every workout with my training partner, Connor Revord, and hoped that training with him would only make us both stronger runners during the season. I wanted to hit the same marks that he made and also move up towards the best in Florida. For me, I got to train with one of the top runners in the country; for Connor, he got to run with an extremely reliable and consistent training partner who could push him to excel.

Training Program

In addition to our annual cross country camp at Appalachian State University, I had the opportunity to attend Jay Johnson's Boulder Running Camp at the University of Colorado. This season especially, while continuing to train on hilly courses throughout the season, I tried to run my workouts during hotter weather in an attempt to simulate the brutal racing conditions common in Florida. During my sophomore and junior years, I felt sluggish during the State Championship at Little Everglades because of the heat and the hills. Therefore, I wanted to be much more prepared during my senior year by adapting my body to much tougher racing conditions.

Here is how my training for my senior cross country season differed from my junior cross country season, with details of my training sessions provided in Chapter 7:

(Training Paces)

Year	5K PR	5K racing range	Median race pace	Tempo	Steady	Easy
9th	17:32	18:00 – 18:30	5:55	6:25	7:15	7:45
10th	16:55	17:20 – 17:40	5:40	5:55	6:25	7:15
11th	16:12	16:25 – 16:40	5:20	5:40	5:55	6:25
12th	15:44	15:50 – 16:05	5:06	5:20	5:40	5:55

- **Easy:** Distances increased to 8-9 miles, with long runs occurring every week of the season. Pace was usually progressive, peaking out at sub-6:00 pace per mile.
- **Steady**: Distances now 5-6 miles of steady running, with pace improving to about 5:40 pace per mile. Striders were now on every-other day.
- **Tempo:** Distances continued to be the same as steady runs; pace improved as well (5:20 pace per mile). Longer cool downs afterwards.
- **Interval:** Split times getting much faster; recovery times were now vital. Integration of thresh-hold workouts to work on running "comfortably hard." Also, tried to simulate race conditions, since mid-morning races at the

end of the season would consist of extreme heat. Workouts were much longer, with shorter speed at the end of workouts. No more breaks midway through workouts.

Doing the Little Things… Getting That Slight Edge

Since swimming proved to be so successful during my junior track season, I continued this form of cross training throughout my senior year. But it's more than doing this type of extra training that made a significant difference. It was a combination of keeping my running and swimming workouts up along with: weights (3 times a week), indoor rock climbing (once or twice a week), push-ups and core drills (every night), and stretching (before and after every practice).

A New Season Plan

In Florida, the cross country season is much longer than the track season (6 months as compared to 4 months). Therefore, you MUST have a plan during cross country season to be consistent. My senior cross country season was certainly the most consistent season for me; I ran in a very tight range based on time, even though the courses varied significantly in difficulty. This showed that I learned how to race a certain time no matter what the conditions were.

This cross country season was when I finally realized how to plan out each training section within a season. During my freshman year, I planned out an easy-base, mixed with some steady and tempo running. There were no "finals" per se, since I didn't get to run at the State Championship. Sophomore year was similar to freshman year, with the exception that I did get to run at the State Championship. Junior year was much more systematic, breaking the seasons into sub-categories (easy-base, steady-base, tempo training, and racing season), but this approach caused the team to peak too early. However, by my senior year cross country season, this was how we planned out the different parts of the season:

- Easy-base
- Steady-base
- Hills-tempo
- Competition-prep
- Competition
- Finals

Making Some Noise

In my first race of the season, I blazed to a PR of 15:47 at the Red Mule 5K. Finishing in 3rd place in a very deep high school field, I edged out my friend and Florida Southern College alum Lee Stephens. Lee, who is a running legend in the Tampa area, has a PR of 15:38 and is consistently between 15:40 – 15:50 every race. What impressed me the most was my kick, where I managed to beat someone I had never beaten before. Also, I raced an extremely consistent race; my splits for the mile marks were 5:00, 5:10, and 5:00.

After an off-day at UF's very slow course in Gainesville the following week, I ran a solid 16:07 at the FSU Invitational. Placing 6th, I raced against some of the top runners in the state and only came in behind runners ranked either #1 or #2 in their respective classifications. My kick was strong once again in this race, as I moved from 9th to 6th in the last 400m. Not only did I finish with about a 1:30 improvement from my sophomore year effort, but I helped Jesuit dominate the team standings in this prestigious invitational.

Further Recognition

A few days later, the St. Pete Times started to take note that I was emerging as one of the best runners in Hillsborough County during my senior cross country season. This newspaper published an article that summarized my improvements throughout high school cross country, and how my artwork helped "illustrate" this improvement.

St. Petersburg Times

Published: October 1, 2008

Jesuit Runner a Portrait of Determination

By Keith Niebuhr

TAMPA - Jordan Schilit needed a subject to draw for a project in his advanced placement art class at Jesuit, so he picked himself. In a concentration essay submitted to his instructor, the standout cross country performer described his mission:

"I will depict my life as a runner - both the triumphs and the sorrows that have developed my character. I will illustrate the vigor and difficulty of distance running as well as the excitement gained from when you succeed. My motivation for this idea came from the first-hand experiences of the wide-ranges of emotions that a runner can go through. I may have achieved many significant accomplishments with high school running, but the hunger for an individual and team state championship has motivated me to achieve more than I could have ever imagined."

Schilit hopes his skills as an artist can do justice to his talents as a runner. Drawings, he believes, often tell a story better than words. "Sometimes you have emotions you can't describe," Schilit said. "But you can show them with your artwork." As both an artist and a runner, the senior has come a long way since his freshman year. That fall, Schilit enrolled in an art class because he was required to. He started with simple sketchbook drawings but ultimately was selected for an honors class and later his current course, reserved for the most talented of the lot.

Schilit also began running as a freshman but initially wasn't good enough to make the varsity roster. Last fall, he placed 12th at the Class 2A state meet. Today, he's one of the region's best distance runners, has a personal best of 15 minutes, 47 seconds and almost certainly will run in college. Between art and running, Schilit finds parallels. "You have to be patient with artwork and drawing," Schilit said. "And in cross country, it's not something that just comes to you. (Not making the team as a ninth-grader) taught me that nothing comes easy."

On a highly regarded squad that includes Connor Revord, who is among the state's top performers, Schilit often gets overlooked. But, as Plant's Mike Boza, who coached Schilit two years at Jesuit, put it, "He'd be the No. 1 runner on most teams" in Florida. "He's running with a lot of confidence, knowing he's in the hunt," Boza said. "He's not afraid to run out front in every race. And he tries to win."

http://www.tampabay.com/sports/crosscountrypreps/article833712.ece

Art Follows Life...And Running

On a side note, my art did improve alongside my running. I truly did learn how to go out and lead races and find the toughness to perform at a high level. I wasn't afraid to run with the best in the state this cross country season.

Sure enough, my final statement with my artwork paralleled greatly my feelings towards running as my senior cross country season came to an end. Here is how I described this experience in my AP Art concentration, "My Life as a Runner."

I have found that illustrating my life as a runner through the saddest and happiest events in my career say much more than the stories told about these races. It was meaningful to describe the journey traveled through my distance running so far – from a recreational middle school runner to an average high school runner to one of the top runners in the state of Florida. I have been able to use contrasting of colors in many instances to put the focus on myself and my emotions, rather than simply illustrating a general picture. I have been able to focus on the depression of realizing I am not always fast enough, the agony of losing, the joy of running a personal-best time, and the confidence of being well prepared to succeed. These running emotions may seem like only memories from the past, but they tell a story of how I can improve my life as a better person off the track – an individual who has the indestructible drive to succeed, despite the many setbacks presented along the way. Distance running is my passion; this sport allows me to control my own destiny and makes me feel at peace, allowing me to zone into my own world. I feel that my artwork draws the viewers into that emotional world and lets them wear my shoes on the track as well as along my path to success in the future.

My final art piece (shown at the end of this chapter) truly describes my feelings of running through the end of my cross country season. I feel that I had become "one with the course" and that I had gained the ability to control a race. I had learned what my capabilities were in the past, what they are in the present, and what I hope to accomplish in the future. I felt that my immense improvement in racing itself was the basis of creating that work of art.

Gaining Momentum

After a 16:09 performance at the Pre-State Meet at Little Everglades, it was time for the Hillsborough County Championship. I ran a very smart race, starting out in 8th place for the first mile, moving up to 6ᵗʰ during the second mile, and then finishing with a strong kick to secure 4ᵗʰ place. Not only did I manage to beat Connor Revord for the first time in my high school career, but I placed highly amongst some of the other top runners in Florida as I improved my time from last year by 40 seconds, with a 15:56 on a very difficult course.

We returned to Lake Park the following week for the 2A District 5 Championship. Towards the end of the race, Connor had to stop due to a stomach illness, so I picked up the slack and ran for the win. The course was quite a bit long so my 16:08 winning time, which was over 20 seconds ahead of the 2ⁿᵈ place finisher, was a significant accomplishment.

St. Petersburg Times
Published: November 6, 2008

2A-5 Cross Country: Jesuit Prevails
One Tiger Goes Down, Another Takes His Place
By Keith Niebuhr

LUTZ — Jesuit's Jordan Schilit has spent much of his prep career in the shadows of teammate Connor Revord. But on Thursday, Schilit took center stage. When Revord succumbed to a minor stomach ailment in the final mile of the 2A-5 meet at Lake Park, Schilit stepped up to take the title and lead his team to a resounding win. "It feels great," Schilit said. "I ran pretty well."

Schilit, who finished in 16:08, was one of five Tigers in the top eight. Jesuit's 23 points was well ahead of Robinson (78) and Frostproof (84). After Schilit, Jesuit's best finishes were by Logan Trimble (third, 16:51) and Blake Lopez (fifth, 17:05). Revord led the race before taking ill (he still finished 50th), but Schilit, who was trailing by only about five to 10 seconds, seized on the opportunity. Minutes after taking the lead, he crossed the finish 23 seconds before Sebring's Conner Bauer. "If it wasn't me, I'm glad it was him," Revord said. "He works harder than anyone I know."

Boys team scores — Jesuit 23, Robinson 78, Frostproof 84, Bartow 116 Individual Leaders — Schilit (Jes) 16:08, Bauer (Seb) 16:31, Trimble (Jes) 16:51, Probst (CCC) 17:02, Lopez (Jes) 17:05, Parker (Jes) 17:06, Kempton (Fp) 17:09, Martin (Jes) 17:16, Rivard (Jes) 17:18, Epperson (Rob) 17:23,

http://www.tampabay.com/sports/crosscountrypreps/article893644.ece?comments=legacy

Racing with Confidence

On November 14th, we traveled to Estero for the 2A Region 3 Championship. Running on the same difficult, yet hotter, course from last year, I definitely showed I was an experienced racer. I started off this race very conservatively, since I was in 7th at the mile and 5th at the 2-mile. With about a ½ mile to go, I moved into 2nd place, and held on to that position for the remainder of the race. I split 5:15 for the last mile, which was faster than any other runner in that field and was good enough to bring me within 10 seconds of Connor.

Tampa Jesuit vs. Belen Jesuit

The following Saturday, we were ready to prove ourselves worthy of a 2A State Championship trophy. We predicted that if we had all of our top-5 under 16:30, then we would be able to defeat 2-time defending State Champs Belen Jesuit; however, they were completely unstoppable that morning.

I stuck to my conservative game plan of simply going out with the pack and not pushing the pace. I wasn't even in the top-20 runners by the half-way point, but worked my way up the entire race until I had locked-up 7th place by the time I finished. My 15:55 effort was a strong performance, since I was only 3 seconds behind Connor and improved on last year's time at Little Everglades by almost 50 seconds; however, it wasn't quite as strong as Tampa Jesuit truly needed.

As a team, we averaged 16:05 per runner, since Ben Martin, Connor Rivard, and Blake Lopez all ran PRs by over 40 seconds – truly the way to compete at the State Championship. Meanwhile, I didn't even run a PR. I ran a solid, but not an outstanding race, which is what the team needed to place 2nd overall. But, the rest of the team transcended all expectations and enabled us to run the fastest team average in Jesuit cross country history, and with only a 26 second spread for 1-5. I, on the other hand, didn't quite have the confidence to run with the leaders and go for that breakthrough performance, like the rest of our team had accomplished.

The Tampa Tribune
Published: November 23, 2008

Stellar Jesuit Takes Second
By: Bill Ward

To have any hope of winning the boys Class 2A state title, the members of Jesuit's cross country team knew each of them would have to turn in a lifetime best showing - or come awfully close to one.

To the man, that's what the Tigers did Saturday at Little Everglades Ranch. Only problem was their rival, No. 1-ranked Miami Belen Jesuit, ran nearly as well to win its third consecutive state crown. This time, Belen edged Jesuit by just 16 points.

But considering how far this Jesuit team has come this fall - particularly since last month's Pre State Invitational, where the Tigers finished fifth overall and third among 2A schools - Saturday's performance arguably ranks among the ones they turned in for their four state titles.

"I'm sure everyone thought Belen would beat us by 50 points or more," Tigers senior Jordan Schilit said. "We just wanted to show the team we could be and make them earn it."

Belen, which now owns four state titles, certainly did. The Wolverines needed to put all five of their scorers in the top 20 - an extremely difficult feat at the state finals - to get past a senior-heavy Tigers team that peaked perfectly under Coach Greg Maurin.

Jesuit's top two runners, Connor Revord and Schilit, were there in the top 10 as usual. Revord grabbed sixth place in a 5-kilometer time of 15 minutes, 52 seconds, and Schilit was just one place and three seconds behind him.

http://www2.tbo.com/content/2008/nov/23/sp-stellar-jesuit-takes-second/

Redemption...But Not Perfection

After coming so close (15 points) to Belen Jesuit at the State Championship, we decided that one last shot at beating Florida's main powerhouse was certainly within our grasp. So, we thought that the Nike Cross Nationals Regional qualifier would be a perfect opportunity to make some noise at the national level.

On the very hilly and challenging SAS Soccer Complex course in Cary, North Carolina, I had a near-breakout performance with my 16:06 effort, placing 34th in this Southeast-USA Regional Championship. Times ran about 20 seconds slow from Little Everglades performances, so finishing in the low-16 range was a great accomplishment for me. However, I would have liked to have hung on with the sub-15:50 crowd for more of the last mile; it was only that final hill that prevented this race from being a breakout performance for me. Nonetheless, my more respectable racing this week helped the team edge out Belen Jesuit by 4 points.

Then, only a few days later, I raced in a time trial on Jesuit's track. Although the weather was very nice, it was plenty windy and I had to run the majority of this race on my own. Almost all of my races this cross country season were against very competitive fields, so to lower my PR to 15:44 when basically running by myself was yet another example of how consistent I had become this cross country season.

It was my consistency, not breakthrough performances, during my senior cross country season that that helped me make the All-Hillsborough Cross Country First Team.

The Tampa Tribune
Published: December 21, 2008

The Tampa Tribune's All-Hillsborough County Cross Country Team

By: *Bill Ward*

BOYS FIRST TEAM

John Grellner, Sr., Wharton - Solid performer all season with top-three finishes in his 3A district and regional meets; sixth at county championships

John Mitchell, Sr., Durant - Overcame early-season cramping problem to turn in top-five finishes at county, as well as 4A district and regional finals.

Mark Parrish, Jr., Chamberlain - For second consecutive year, was the county's top performer when it mattered most with strong third-place finish in 3A state finals.

Connor Revord, Sr., Jesuit - Led Tigers to state runners-up trophy; won second consecutive individual 2A regional crown

Jordan Schilit, Sr., Jesuit - One of the area's most consistent performers, taking fourth in the county meet, winning his 2A district and finishing second in the regional.

Derek Wehunt, Sr., Sickles - County champion for second consecutive year; set course record by winning flrunners.com Invitational

Trenor Wilkins, Jr., Plant - Panthers' No. 1 man had a breakout season, taking third in county meet and winning his first individual 3A regional title

http://www2.tbo.com/content/2008/dec/21/sp-the-tampa-tribunes-all-hillsborough-county-cros/

Senior Year Cross Country (5K) Results (2008):

Date	Race Name	Venue	5K Result
08/30/08	Red Mule 5K	McKethan Lake	**15:47**
09/20/08	UF Gator Invite	UF Golf Course	16:36
09/27/08	FSU Invitational	Miccosukee Greenway	16:07
10/18/08	Pre-State Meet	Little Everglades	16:09
10/28/08	Hills. County Championship	Lake Park	15:56
11/03/08	District Championship	Lake Park	16:08
11/14/08	Regional Championship	Estero Comm. Park	16:36
11/22/08	State Championship	Little Everglades	15:55
11/29/08	NXN Southeast Championship	SAS Soccer Complex (NC)	16:06

In addition, I raced a 5000m time trial on Jesuit's outdoor track.

Date	Race Name	5000m Result
12/02/08	5000m Time Trial at JHS	**15:44**

* * * * * * *

This was a great cross country season for me – breaking 16:00 in the 5K, winning Districts, and having great showings on difficult courses at the County and District Championships and NXN southeast. In addition, I continued my improvement as I had done the prior four years, this time lowering my 5K times from my junior year by an average of about a ½ minute. I was now one of the elite runners in the state. I was proud of my efforts and of my results and I was psyched for track.

Track 2009

> **Maximum Mileage: 55**
> **Average Mileage: 40**

Introduction

During my last season of high school running, I wanted to have no regrets. I wanted to look back at every race and say that I was 100% satisfied with my efforts, even if improvement was still evident. I wanted to utilize more speed training this season and wanted to make my mark as among the top track runners in Florida, hopefully taking down some records along the way.

Training Program

Here is how my training for my senior track season differed from my senior cross country season, with details of my training sessions provided in Chapter 7:

- **Easy:** Same distances and essentially the same pacing.
- **Steady**: Distances now 6 miles of steady running; same paces. Striders were very common and working on short turnover after distance was key.
- **Tempo:** Distances and paces were same, but tempo running was not as common as intervals. Tempos mainly occurred at beginning of season. Cool downs continued to increase in distance.
- **Interval:** Split times now tried to simulate racing paces and were very difficult with such short recovery times. Continued thresh-hold, but with even longer distances. One key factor was running several 200m repeats (all at sub-:30) after speed workouts were completed. Really worked on turnover this season in order to make my kick very strong.

No Sign of Slowing Down

On February 18th, just as the track season was getting underway, I felt some pain in my hip. I didn't think too much of it, and assumed it was simply soreness or tightness. I woke up the next morning, however, in excruciating pain and it seemed to worsen as the day progressed. Nonetheless, I toughened it out for Jesuit's Blue/White Meet and still managed to run a 13-second PR of 4:33 in the 1600m. I knew that I would be able to run significantly faster than that if I was feeling 100% and would therefore be able to stay within striking range of my close friend Connor Revord, who was the #1 contender for the State Championship in the 1600m.

It turns out that I needed to see a doctor for the next two weeks, who was able to get my hip re-aligned. The doctor said that this slight misalignment of my hip was probably from over-compensation of my left foot, since my right foot had a stress fracture during junior track season.

Sure enough, I felt ready to go out and PR and make my name known around the state by the time our first inter-squad meets rolled around. On March 11th (my mom's 50th birthday), Jesuit hosted one of the strongest and deepest 800m fields all year. I would be running in a new event for myself – the 800m – as I was always characterized as a distance runner with sub-par leg turnover. With only Jesuit, Sickles and Robinson competing, this chilly evening accounted for three school records, four runners going under 1:55, seven going under 2:00, and many more PRs. I managed to come in 6th place, out-kicking my friend and teammate Mike McEnany in the final 50m for a new PR – 1:59.50. I was so glad to come through in 3rd place on my team in this race and to prove that I was in contention for a spot on our 4x800m team, which would certainly contend for a State Championship title.

My Own Rhythm

Only two days later, I competed in the 5000m at Nike Indoor Nationals in Boston. After watching freshman phenom Lucas Verzbicas run a 14:18 completely unchallenged, I thought to myself that I should be able to run in the same dominating style, even if I was not nearly as fast. In the third heat of the

5000m on Friday night, I decided that I would have to take command and run "my own race" if I wanted a shot at All-American status. I led the heat for the initial two miles, splitting 4:46 and 5:00; it wasn't until the last mile that I was over-taken by All-American Brian Faherty. Nonetheless, my PR of 15:33 was a solid 11-second improvement – competitive enough for a 16th place finish. Finishing 16th overall in national competition, I was thrilled with my time and realized that I would eventually be able to hang on to such a pace, since I hadn't even done much speed work thus far this season. I knew that I was in control of that race, and trying to control more races in the future would only make me a more competitive runner this track season.

Kicking for the Win…Again and Again

For our first major race of the season, we traveled to Jacksonville for the very prestigious Bob Hayes Invitational. Even though, earlier in the day, I ran a 2:02 split to help the 4x800m relay place 2nd, my highlight of the day was surely the 3200m. I didn't have the fastest seed in this highly competitive field, but I felt it was necessary to lead the entire first mile. By lap 7 I had faded to 5th place, but I kept my composure and managed a 1:07 last 400m to take 1st place by 3 seconds. Despite over 30 mph winds, I managed to run a new PR of 9:44, which would equate to a sub-9:30 effort under less severe conditions. It was at this time that I realized my kick could be used to my advantage and could pull some surprises this season as the meets gained even more prestige.

I was even more of an under-dog as the team traveled to Tallahassee for the FSU Invitational; my 9:44 PR was only good enough for the #15 seed in what would be considered one of the fastest and deepest 3200m fields in Florida history. Not only was wind a factor this week, but a 3-hour rain delay produced a very swampy track indeed. None seemed to be fazed, however, as I came across the 1600m mark in 4:41 (9th place). I got distanced by the group of sub-9:20 guys, but still managed to run another PR -- 9:31. My kick was strong once again, as I ran a 1:06 last lap.

But maybe the most impressive of my "kicks" through this point in the season came the following week at the University of Florida Invitational. Although, I was put in the second-fastest heat of the 1600m, I wanted to prove the true section in which I belonged. I led a tight group through 1200m in 3:20, but was then passed by a few runners during the next 150m. I stayed right behind them and not only passed them during the last 200m, but won by over 3 seconds with my 1:04 last lap. My new PR of 4:24 beat some runners in the fast heat (11th overall) and may have been even faster if I was running in the faster section. Then, I returned to the track the following morning for the 4x1600m relay. As the third leg for Jesuit, I received the baton 100m behind Hunter Hayes – Bishop Kenny's third leg. Nonetheless, I managed to close the gap by a few seconds each lap, and then ran a sensational last 400m in 1:00. Despite running under the mid-day Florida sun in extreme heat, I was only 3 seconds off my new PR – good enough for the fourth-fastest split out of any runner in the race. I gave the baton to Connor Revord with a couple seconds of cushion too, and it proved to be the difference-maker in our 18:02 4x1600m 1st place finish.

In the Hunt

On April 11th, at the UT Distance Carnival, I was ready to run yet another PR in the 3200m under perfect weather conditions. I led the first 800m of this race, but I proved my dominance over the field after a 1:06 third lap, distancing the field by close to 10 seconds at that point. I never looked back as I crushed my previous 3200m, running a time that would remain as among the top-7 in Florida for the 2009 outdoor season. My 9:22 not only won this race by 15 seconds, but was faster than the winning time from the 2008 2A FHSAA Track State Finals.

I now had the confidence that I could run speedy times, even when doing all of the work in a race on my own. I could only imagine how many seconds I would be able to shave off my 3200m time if I was entered in another stacked field of racers. Yes, I got to run in that 3200m race at the FSU Invitational, but I didn't have nearly as much confidence as I had during my race at the UT Distance Carnival. I knew I was in the hunt for a 3200m state title in a few weeks and even more so, an individual who could be a major point contributor for my team.

Racking Up the Points in Districts …

The following week at the 2A District 9 Championship, the temperatures were hot as usual for the 4x800m relay. For some reason, there was still talk that maybe I shouldn't be running on that relay squad, simply because I had been labeled as the DISTANCE runner. After 2:01 and 2:02 splits by legs #1 and #2 respectively, I showed my consistency by running a relay-PR 2:00 split. I passed the baton to Connor with plenty of room ahead of 2nd place, and he easily anchored our relay team to victory.

Then, it was time for the individual events. In the 1600m, my plan was to pace our #3 guy for the first 1200m, so I ran 1:12, 1:10, 1:09 as I sat with him just outside of the top-10. But as we approached 400m to go, I surged to the front and ran another phenomenal kick of 1:00, finishing just 1 second behind Connor. In the end, it was a Jesuit sweep of Connor, me, and sophomore Blake Lopez – taking 1st, 2nd, and 3rd respectively. Later in the evening, I cruised to a victory in the 3200m with a 9:45, recording 4:51 and 4:54 splits. Perhaps most important, Jesuit High School won its 10th District title in 11 years.

… and in Regions

I had plenty of momentum going into the 2A Region 3 Championship and certainly didn't show any signs of slowing down. In my first race of the day, under terrible conditions due to forest fires in south Florida, I lowered my PR for a 4x800m split once again to 1:58. By resting Connor, the relay didn't win this week, but we were confident for next week's race, with Connor back in the lineup.

During the individual events in the evening, I once again paced our extremely talented sophomore, Blake Lopez, with the hope of getting him to advance for the following week. With a strong field of runners capable of running sub 4:30 1600m times, which is a few seconds faster than his PR, Blake began to fade at around the 1200m mark, so I picked up my pace in order to maximize our team's points. Not only did I move up from 5th to 2nd during the last 400m, but my :59 split was fast enough to give me a new PR – 4:23. Shortly afterwards, I cruised once again to a 3200m victory, this time in 9:42, giving Jesuit's 71 points in the Regional meet – enough for 1st place.

The Tampa Tribune
Published: April 25, 2009

Track: Jesuit Boys Win Region Meet
Tribune Staff Report

Riding strong performances by senior distance stars Connor Revord and Jordan Schilit, the Jesuit boys track and field team outlasted host Naples Golden Gate on Friday to win the Class 2A-Region 3 meet.

Revord won the 1,600 and finished second in the 800, while Schilit qualified for next week's state meet in three events - winning the 3,200 and placing second in the 1,600 and as a member of the Tigers' 4x800 relay team.

"The guys did well," said Jesuit coach Ray Rodriguez. "I think we've got a shot to finish in the top four at states. We've got a great bunch of kids. They always seem to put it out there in situations when we need them."

CLASS 2-A, REGION 3 BOYS TRACK
1. Jesuit (J) 78, 2. Golden Gate (GG) 68, 3. Nature Coast (NC) 54
4x800: 1. Robinson (Bryan Garcia, Terril Gibson, Mike Shuey, Darrin Gibson) 8:02.35, **2. Jesuit (Logan Trimble, Jordan Schilit, Joe Parker, Mike McEnany)** 8:02.53, 3. Astronaut 8:14.09, 4. Nature Coast 8:15.21
1600: 1. Connor Revord (J) 4:19.42, **2. Jordan Schilit (J) 4:23.02**, 3. Bruce Federico (NC) 4:25.98, 4. Tyler Davidson (CB) 4:26.67
3200: **1. Jordan Schilit (J) 9:42.21**, 2. Sean Quinn (BV) 9:51.42, 3. Tyler Davidson (CB) 9:52.69, 4. Argeo Cruz (I) 9:53.11

http://www2.tbo.com/content/2009/apr/25/sp-jesuit-boys-win-region-track-meet/

©2009 Media General Inc. All Rights Reserved.

A Flawless Finale

Under the blistering 95 degree temperatures on the afternoon of May 2nd, I stepped onto Winter Park High School's track with hopes of winning my first State Championship of my high school career. I knew I was the difference maker for the 4x800m squad, since the other 3 guys all ran this relay at the 2008 FHSAA State Track Finals last year. I had proven myself worthy of a spot on this relay team and today was my day to show that I could come through when my team needed me the most.

After strong legs by Mike McEnany (1:56) and Logan Trimble (1:57), I knew I had to keep the tempo fast if we wanted to be on par for our school record. "Mac" and Logan had given me a comfortable lead of about 100m, and I maintained that same lead when I passed the baton to Connor Revord with my 1:58 split. Connor anchored in 1:55 to secure our victory, which was a new school record of 7:47.87 (2009 then-US #6). The four seniors on our 4x800m team will continue running in college: Mike McEnany will run for Wake Forest, Logan Trimble will run for MIT, Connor Revord will run for Penn State, and I will run for Haverford.

Later in the evening, the individual event finals began. As I stepped up to the line for the 1600m, most spectators expected me to step off the track in order to run a fresh 3200m. Not only did I prove otherwise, but I ran one of my best races in my high school career. The pace was slow from the start, with a 2:20 first 800m split. But as I moved up from 9th place to 3rd place with 450m to go, I tapped Connor on the shoulder and told him that we "needed to go now." The two of us took off with Belen Jesuit's Joseph Dorfman just ahead of us. We blazed by him and stayed ahead of the rest of the field as Connor and I finished 1-2 at the finish. Only 1 second behind Connor, I split 2:02 for my last 800m and 0:58 for my last 400m. This race was surely tactical, but in the end, it was the experienced runners who proved victorious. Nonetheless, I still pulled off a PR of 4:22 during this wild race, and only imagined how fast I could run the mile in the future if I was going for a fast time and didn't have to worry about two other races.

Afterwards, in the 3200m, I was pretty tired from my efforts during my other two races, but I knew that I had to hang onto one of the top few places in order to give Jesuit enough points for the State Runner-Up trophy. I actually pushed the pace for the first 1600m, but that was only to ensure that I would be in the top-2 after many runners had faded. Even though I had once had thoughts that it would be crazy to give up an individual title for two 2nd place finishes, I had a different mindset on that day. Once I heard the gun shot during the 1600m, I realized that my purpose during the State Championship was to bring home glory for the team – not as an individual. Yes, I gave up my shot of going fresh against a fresh-9:11 3200m runner (Colin Barker); however, as the meet culminated, I walked away with 3 medals (one gold and two silvers) that I had earned for my own benefit, and a more important silver medal that I had earned for my team.

St. Petersburg Times
Published: May 3, 2009

Game Jesuit Takes Second
By Izzy Gould

WINTER PARK — Connor Revord felt something brush his back and worried the trailing runners had tumbled like bowling pins. The Jesuit senior turned his head and caught a glimpse of teammate Jordan Schilit during the final lap of the 1,600-meter run. "I saw some people moving up and I tapped him," Schilit said. "I said, 'We've got to go.' " The pair of Tigers reached deep and put together a one-two finish to pile on more team points for Jesuit. Revord had claimed his first individual state title, and as hopes of claiming a team championship began to fade, each strong distance performance made securing second place a reality.

Jesuit finished with 47 points, falling only to Monsignor Pace, which won Saturday's Class 2A state meet at Showalter Field with 82. Archbishop McCarthy was third (42). "I'm very satisfied because Monsignor Pace should have been Monster Pace," Jesuit coach Ray Rodriguez said with a laugh. "They were very good, every single one of them."

Jesuit's day began with a state title in the 4x800, the third time Revord ran on a state-title 4x800 relay. This time he ran with Mike McEnany, Logan Trimble and Schilit, shattering the school record by seven seconds (7 minutes, 47.87 seconds). Schilit had talked about dropping out of the 1,600 to focus his energy on the 3,200, but after the 4x800 win he changed his mind. He claimed second place in the 1,600 and 3,200, and though he didn't win an individual title, he gave the Tigers their best chance to claim the team crown. "We would not be grabbing a big trophy if he didn't stick his neck out and run the 1,600," Rodriguez said. "That was huge."

http://www.tampabay.com/sports/tranckandfieldpreps/article997631.ece

I remembered last year how I had been so lucky to even run at the State Championship, scoring only 3 points. But during my senior year, I maximized my scoring capabilities with 26 points, which is why I was awarded Jesuit High School's 2009 Most Valuable Player for the track team. And it was Coach Rodriguez's idea in the first place that allowed him to win the 2009 All-Hillsborough County Coach of the Year.

More Recognition

In April of 2009, I was selected by DyeStat.com for its new "Deep Roster" feature. DyeStat, known as "The Internet Home of High School Track & Field," describes their selection process below:

__Deep Roster__ is a feature on DyeStat in which we seek to recognize the efforts and achievements of those athletes who <u>might not normally be featured in the headlines on our site</u>. There are standout athletes all over the place, many deep rosters of talent, and we want to start recognizing some of these committed student athletes each week.

Jordan Schilit, Sr - Tampa Jesuit HS - Tampa FL - As a freshman, Jordan failed to make Jesuit's state championship varsity XC squad. However, he steadily improved his 5K time during his career, from 18:30 to 17:30 to 16:30, and finally to 15:30. He rose from being the team's #10 runner all the way to a top-16 finisher at this year's NIN in the 5k. His 3200 has dropped from 11:10 to 9:31 since his freshman year, and he hopes to make a run for his first state championship May 2nd. Never the star, he's nonetheless emerged as the team's leader. *Submitted by Coach David Revord*

My performance at the 2009 FHSAA State Track Finals was a dream come true; I won my first State Championship and also took home 3 State Runner-Up Medals. I was soon thereafter featured with Connor Revord on the front page of DyeStat.com for our 4x800m relay victory. I am the only person to ever be included in both DyeStat's "Deep Roster" and its homepage.

In addition, the St. Pete Times took note of both my consistency throughout the season and my outstanding performances at the State Championship, thus, rewarding me with First Team All-Hillsborough County honors in what was considered to be the most competitive track season in Hillsborough County history.

St. Petersburg Times
Published: June 4, 2009

All-Hillsborough County Boys Track

By Eduardo A. Encina

Track athlete of the Year: Dentarius Locke, Chamberlain, Sr.

Coach of the Year: Ray Rodriguez, Jesuit

First Team

100, Locke: Set a PR in the region meet with a 10.31, then set a state record at the 4A meet.

200, Locke: Dusted the field and set a state record in the 3A semis (20.58), then sealed gold in the final (21.42).

400, Markais Neal, Sr., Armwood: County's top state finisher placed sixth at the 3A meet.

800, John Mitchell, Sr., Durant: UF recruit was one of three county state champs in the event, but the only to break the 1:53 mark.

1,600, Connor Revord, Sr., Jesuit: Won a 2A state title — his first individual title — with a 4:21.51.

3,200, Jordan Schilit, Sr., Jesuit: Second in the 2A state meet.

4x800 relay, Sickles (Marc DeJute, Daniel Wehunt, Derek Wehunt, Julian Gines): Won the Class 4A state title.

4x400 relay, Wharton (Chris Watson, Nick Swain, Sean Obinwa, Kevin Williams): Placed third in the Class 3A state meet after losing to Armwood in regionals.

4x100 relay, Wharton (Kyle Wilcox, Shane McEwen, Chris Watson, Kevin Williams): District champions were also state qualifiers, placing 10th in 3A state prelims after placing third in regionals.

http://www.tampabay.com/sports/tranckandfieldpreps/article1007124.ece

Senior Year Track Results (2009):

Before the outdoor season, I traveled up to Nike Indoor Nationals to run the 5000m on a banked indoor track.

Date	Race Name	5000m (indoors)
03/13/09	Nike Indoor Nationals	**15:33**

Date	Race Name	800m	1600m	3200m
02/19/09	Jesuit Blue/ White Meet		4:33	
03/11/09	Jesuit Tri-Meet	**1:59**		
03/21/09	Bob Hayes Invitational			9:44
03/27/09	FSU Relays	2:03		9:31
04/03/09	UF Relays		4:24	
04/11/09	UT Distance Carnival			**9:22**
04/16/09	District Championship		4:31	9:45
04/24/09	Regional Championship		4:23	9:42
04/16/09	State Championship		**4:22**	9:43

In addition, I competed in several relays this year. This was the first time that I had the opportunity to run in any relay events. I competed in the following 4x800m races (which, by the way, are always run BEFORE the 1600m and 3200m races):

Date	Race Name	Relay Split	Team Time
03/21/09	Bob Hayes Invitational	2:02	8:17
04/16/09	District Championship	2:00	8:02
04/24/09	Regional Championship	1:58	8:02
05/02/09	State Championship	**1:58**	7:47

Also, Jesuit put together a 4x1600m relay team at the UF Relays.

Date	Race Name	Relay Split	Team Time
04/03/09	UF Relays	4:27	18:01

* * * * * *

In light of Jesuit's motto "Men for Others," I consider my performance at the State Championship to be my most significant non-academic accomplishment during high school. During my senior year, I finished my high school running career with the goals that I had hoped for as a freshman. I led the cross country team to a State Runner-Up team performance that had a team average fast enough to win any prior year in Florida history. I not only was team captain of the best cross country team in school history, but also led the Jesuit track team to a State Runner-Up team performance in 2009. I won a State Championship on the 4x800m relay team, which ran 7:47.87 – a new school record and 6th fastest performance in the USA at that time for 2009. Also, instead of dropping out of the 1600m for an attempted 3200m title, my State Runner-Up finishes in the 1600m and 3200m gave Jesuit High School enough points to place 2nd overall as a team. What a rewarding way to finish my high school career.

In terms of improvement, I increased by the usual 3 VDOT levels in my senior year:

- I went from a relatively slow 800m runner to a sub-2:00 runner; my PR of 1:58 (for an event that I had been running for only 7 weeks) was among the 10 fastest times in 2A.
- Although I didn't race the 1600m during my junior year, I improved my 1600m time by more than 20 seconds from sophomore year; my PR was top-10 in Florida.
- I improved my 3200m PR by 23 seconds, and improved my times in 6 consecutive races (and lowered or came within 1 second of my prior race time in 8 out of 9 consecutive races) going back to my junior year. That is unheard of improvement for an elite runner. In addition, my PR of 9:22 was ranked 7th out of all Florida runners.

My PRs in the 800m, 1600m, and 3200m are all times in which any collegiate coach would have an interest. Furthermore, my performance at the State Championship meet itself showed that I am of more value than just running my PRs – I would rather sacrifice individual championships for a team championship. At the 2A Finals, I made the ultimate sacrifice for my team, allowing Jesuit to earn a runner-up trophy at States.

The other Jesuit seniors and I leading the front pack at the UF Gator Invite

Rounding the last turn at the FSU Invitational — the first race I sported the head band

Finishing at the 2008 Hillsborough County Championship; this was my first race in which I finished in front of Connor Revord

My art piece entitled "Cultivated Confidence" won Best of Show at Jesuit High School

The final art piece of my AP Art portfolio described how I felt I had become "one with the course" and that I had the ability to control a race. This mindset helped me significantly during the 2009 outdoor track season

Surging up the final hill at the State Championship during my senior year; I finished 7th. Photo courtesy of Bill Ward of the *Tampa Tribune*

Standing on the awards podium with my first and only cross country individual scoring medal; I led Jesuit to a State Runner-Up finish

Standing with future Haverford teammate Atticus Brigham at Nike Indoor Nationals

Leading my heat of the Nike Indoor Nationals 5000m Final; I placed 16th overall with a new PR of 15:33, finishing 16 seconds off of All-American status

Finally realizing how to kick at the 2009 Bob Hayes Invitational. Photo courtesy of *flrunners.com*

Running the 3200m at FSU in one of the strongest and deepest fields in Florida history; I PR-ed in the 3200m with 9:31. Photo courtesy of *flruners.com*

Running solo – with my feet off the ground – for yet another PR in the 3200m (9:22); I beat the 2nd place finisher by 15 seconds and moved up to the 2nd-fastest time in 2A for the 2009 outdoor season. Photo courtesy of *flrunners.com*

Kicking with Connor Revord after a very tactical 1600m race at Districts. Photo courtesy of Marie Martin

Cruising to my first District crown in track, even after running in both the 4x800m and 1600m earlier in the day. Photo courtesy of Bill Ward of the *Tampa Tribune*

Running my final track workout at Jesuit High School.
Photo courtesy of Bill Ward of the *Tampa Tribune*

The record-breaking Jesuit 4x800m State Champion Relay Team; from left to right: Mac, Logan, me, and Connor

The 4x800 moms; from left to right: my mom, Mrs. Trimble, Mrs. Revord, and Mrs. "Mac"

The 4x800m relay squad, joined by alternate Joe Parker and Coaches Ray Rodriguez and Dave Revord

Sweeping 1-2 with Connor in the 1600m at the 2A State Finals; my 2:02 last 800m and 0:58 last 400m was good enough for a new PR of 4:22. Photo courtesy of Bill Ward of the *Tampa Tribune*

All smiles after reclaiming the State Runner-Up Trophy for Jesuit High School. Photo courtesy of Bill Ward of the *Tampa Tribune*

Our last "skinny guys" picture for the class of 2009 at our senior year track banquet; I'm no longer labeled as the "little guy"

On Your Mark
How YOU Can Lead YOUR Team

I was recently in Salt Lake City, the site of the 2002 Winter Olympic Games, and was reminded of the Olympic motto – "Bigger, Stronger, Faster." That motto effectively summarizes my high school running career:

Yr.	Wt. – yr. start	Wt. – yr. end	Avg. Miles – CC	Max. Miles – CC	Avg. Miles – Track	Max. Miles – Track	5K Race· Pace
9th	80	98	30	38	30	38	5:55
10th	105	116	34	43	32	40	5:40
11th	119	125	40	59	36	54	5:20
12th	130	137	47	66	40	55	5:06

I know that the summary and chart below keep showing up throughout the book, but they have been essential to my consistent improvement throughout high school:

- The **median race-pace** of my 5K racing range became my **tempo pace** for the following year
- The tempo pace became my **steady pace** for the following year
- The steady pace became my **easy pace** for the following year

This basic formula followed me over all four years of my high school career. Below is the visual representation of my racing paces as well as my training – i.e., tempo, steady, and easy – paces during the cross country seasons:

		5K racing range	Median race pace			*(Training Paces)*
Year	*5K PR*			*Tempo*	*Steady*	*Easy*
9th	17:32	18:00 – 18:30	5:55	6:25	7:15	7:45
10th	16:55	17:20 – 17:40	5:40	5:55	6:25	7:15
11th	16:12	16:25 – 16:40	5:20	5:40	5:55	6:25
12th	15:44	15:50 – 16:05	5:06	5:20	5:40	5:55

So, now let me explain in greater detail my systematic approach through both cross country and track during my freshman, sophomore, junior, and senior years. Easy, Steady, and Tempo runs will be summarized. Key Interval workouts from each season will be drawn out more thoroughly. Use the following key when looking at the running charts:

- E= Easy
- S= Steady
- T= Tempo

- I= Interval
- R=Race
- X=Day Off

Note: *Interval workouts during track seasons were almost always run on the track, whereas interval workouts during cross country seasons were run on a variety of different surfaces (i.e. golf courses, roads, trails, soccer fields, and sometimes on the track).*

Over the following pages, I provide details of every running workout during my high school career. Using a running log to jot down any notes after each day's workout, as I did, can only help you look back at each prior season and help you learn what does and doesn't work. Also, note how I have been planning "in the long run"; I have worked very hard to get to where I am today, but I know I will have room for improvement during my collegiate career as well.

Freshman Cross Country – 2005

Maximum Mileage: 38
Average Mileage: 30

Week	Miles	M	Tu	W	Th	F	Sa	Su	Race(s)
1	20	E	X	S	X	E	X	E	
2	23	E	E	X	S	X	E	X	
3	26	S	E	X	E	X	S	X	
4	30	E	S	X	E	X	S	X	
5	35	E	S	X	S	E	S	X	
6	33	E	E	X	S	E	S	X	
7	34	E	S	E	T	E	S	X	
8	36	E	S	E	S	X	S	E	
9	37	E	S	E	E	S	S	X	
10	38	S	E	T	S	E	S	X	
11	35	S	E	T	S	T	E	X	
12	36	E	R	S	T	E	S	X	Time Trial
13	32	I	E	S	T	E	R	X	Red Mule
14	34	I	S	T	E	S	E	X	
15	31	S	T	I	E	R	E	X	USF
16	29	I	E	S	T	E	R	X	FSU
17	32	I	T	E	S	S	E	X	
18	27	I	E	S	E	E	R	X	Flrunners
19	28	S	T	E	S	R	E	X	Postal
20	30	E	R	S	E	T	E	X	Bay Cup
21	33	I	E	S	E	T	S	X	
22	25	E	R	E	S	T	E	X	Districts
23	28	S	E	S	E	T	E	X	
24	26	S	E	S	E	T	E	X	
25	23	T	E	S	E	E	R	X	Footlocker

Training Program

- **Easy:** 4-5 miles either continuous or with a few breaks. Once a week "long runs" of 6-8 miles during the summer base period. Typical pace of 7:30-8:30 per mile.
- **Steady**: Same distances as easy. Either:
  - o start off easy and get progressively faster (i.e. 8:15 pace per mile, then work down to 7:00 per mile); or
  - o a few miles to warm-up, then about 3 miles steady at approximately 7:00 pace per mile, then 1-2 miles to cool-down.
- **Tempo:** Shorter distances than easy or steady, but: 1 mile warm-up, then 2-3 miles at 6:15-6:30 pace per mile, then a cool down of a mile or less.
- **Interval:** These were the speed workouts, which took on a few different forms, as is illustrated below. During freshman year, the focus was primarily on split times for each repetition; eventually, I would learn to run the splits with minimal resting time (i.e., recovery) in between the splits. Here are some sample interval workouts during my freshman cross country season:
  - o "Pyramid of Power" (or "ladder workout") – with 2+ minutes of rest in between each rep and a 2-4 minute break midway through the entire workout (total workout of 3000m):
    - 200m in 0:35
    - 300m in 0:53
    - 400m in 1:11
    - 600m in 1:45
    - 600m in 1:45
    - 400m in 1:10
    - 300m in 0:52
    - 200m in 0:34
  - o 800m Repeats – with 2-3 minutes recovery in between each rep (total workout of 3200m):
    - 4x800m in 2:42, then 2:40, then 2:39, then 2:37
  - o 400m Repeats – with 2:30 recovery in between each rep; 5 minute additional break after 4 reps; another 5 minute rest after 6 reps (total workout of 3200m):
    - 4x400m in 1:08, then 1:10, then 1:12, then 1:12
    - 2x400m in 1:11, then 1:12
    - 2x400m in 1:11, then 1:10

Freshman Track – 2006

Maximum Mileage: 38
Average Mileage: 30

Week	Miles	Workouts M	Tu	W	Th	F	Sa	Su	Race(s)
1	31	E	E	E	E	X	S	X	
2	30	S	E	I	E	E	E	X	
3	38	S	E	T	E	E	S	X	
4	38	S	S	E	T	E	S	X	
5	32	I	S	E	I	E	S	X	
6	34	T	S	E	I	E	E	X	
7	33	I	S	E	I	E	S	X	
8	33	E	R	E	I	E	I	E	Berkeley
9	30	S	I	E	T	E	R	E	Nash Higgins
10	30	S	E	R	E	I	S	X	Leto
11	25	S	I	E	S	E	I	X	
12	30	S	I	E	S	E	S	X	
13	24	E	R	S	I	E	R	X	Chamber; UT
14	29	E	R	S	I	T	S	X	JHS
15	25	E	R	S	T	X	I	E	Districts
16	30	S	S	E	E	X	S	E	
17	26	I	E	S	I	X	S	S	
18	24	I	S	E	S	E	R	X	May Classic

Training Program

- **Easy:** Same distances, but less amount of long runs.
- **Steady:** Slightly faster paces, but same distances.
- **Tempo:** Was more prevalent during track workouts. Faster training and more focused on intervals.
- **Interval:** Slightly faster paces. Recovery times and distances were essentially the same.

During my freshman track season, most of the interval workouts were very similar to those from cross country season. I had not yet developed much leg speed, so workouts were designed for me that could work for both seasons. As I got older, however, workouts became more specific to not only the specific season (i.e. cross country vs. track), but also to the stages of each season (i.e. base, competition-prep, finals, etc…).

"Bigger, Stronger, Faster" – that's what training is all about.

Sophomore Cross Country – 2006

Maximum Mileage: 43
Average Mileage: 34

Week	Miles	Workouts							Race(s)
		M	Tu	W	Th	F	Sa	Su	
1	22	E	E	E	X	E	S	X	
2	25	S	E	S	S	X	T	X	
3	27	S	T	E	S	T	E	X	
4	32	T	S	E	S	X	S	X	
5	35	E	T	S	E	X	S	E	
6	33	T	X	I	S	E	S	X	
7	38	T	S	I	S	E	S	X	
8	35	T	S	I	S	X	E	T	
9	40	E	S	E	T	S	E	X	
10	41	T	E	S	E	S	T	X	
11	42	T	E	S	E	S	I	X	
12	35	T	S	E	R	X	S	E	Time Trial
13	32	T	E	S	S	E	R	X	Red Mule
14	40	T	S	E	I	E	S	X	
15	43	E	I	S	I	X	R	E	LOL
16	40	S	I	S	T	X	R	E	UF
17	39	S	I	S	E	I	X	E	
18	31	S	I	X	E	R	X	E	Flrunners
19	32	X	I	E	T	X	E	S	FSU
20	36	S	I	E	E	R	E	X	Bay Cup
21	33	T	E	S	I	E	R	X	Postal
22	35	I	E	R	E	I	E	X	Districts
23	32	T	S	T	E	R	E	X	Regions
24	20	T	X	E	S	X	R	X	State
25	31	X	E	I	E	E	S	X	
26	27	S	I	E	E	X	R	X	Footlocker

Training Program

- **Easy:** 6-7 miles either continuous or with a few breaks. Once a week "long runs" of 8-10 miles during the summer base period. Typical pace was in the low-7:00 range.
- **Steady:** Same distances as easy. Either:
  - start off easy and get progressively faster (i.e. 7:40 pace per mile, then work down to 6:20 per mile); or
  - a few miles to warm-up, then 3-4 miles steady at 6:25 pace per mile, then 1-2 miles to cool-down.
- **Tempo:** Shorter distances than easy or steady, but: 1 mile warm-up, then 2-3 miles at 5:50-6:05 pace per mile, then a cool down of a mile or less.
- **Interval:** Still focused on split times, but recovery times shortened slightly. More mixing of different distances within workouts, as opposed to repeating the same distances.
  - "Fartlek" Workout – Typically run on a golf course or hilly cross country course. Continuous run for 4 miles total; the "fast" parts should feel like an effort between tempo and interval pace.
    - 3:00 fast, then 3:00 jog
    - 2:00 fast, then 2:00 jog
    - 1:00 fast, then 1:00 jog
    - then, repeat pattern until 4 miles is completed
  - 1200m Repeats – with 2:30 recovery in between reps:
    - 5x1200m in 4:15, then 4:14, then 4:13, then 4:12, then 4:10
    - Also, finish the workout with 8x100m repeats (all at about 0:15-0:16)
  - 1000m Repeats – with less than 2:00 recovery in between reps:
    - 5x1000m in 3:31, then 3:26, then 3:25, then 3:25, then 3:22)
    - Also, finish the workout with some striders in the grass of about 50m each
  - 600m Repeats – with 2:00 recovery in between reps:
    - 8x600m in 1:59, then 1:59, then 1:58, then 1:58, then 1:57, then 1:57, then 1:56, then 1:56)
    - Also, finish with 2x200m in 0:33, then 0:32

Sophomore Track – 2007

> **Maximum Mileage: 40**
> **Average Mileage: 32**

Week	Miles	M	Tu	W	Th	F	Sa	Su	Race(s)
				Workouts					
1	25	E	E	E	X	S	X	E	
2	30	E	X	E	X	S	E	S	
3	37	E	S	E	E	X	S	E	
4	40	E	T	E	I	X	E	S	
5	34	S	T	E	S	X	T	X	
6	37	S	E	S	I	E	E	X	
7	40	S	I	E	I	S	E	X	
8	33	S	T	E	I	X	E	X	
9	35	E	I	E	I	X	E	T	
10	34	X	E	E	I	E	R	E	Steak n' Shake
11	38	S	I	E	T	X	S	I	
12	32	E	I	R	E	E	R	X	JHS; Ch John.
13	30	S	I	E	I	X	R	E	Bob Hayes
14	29	E	S	E	I	E	R	X	UT
15	24	E	R	S	E	R	E	X	Wharton; FSU
16	28	E	I	E	I	S	I	X	
17	31	I	S	E	R	X	T	X	Districts
18	30	I	X	S	E	R	X	E	Spartan Sprint
19	32	S	I	E	T	E	X	I	
20	27	S	I	E	S	E	R	X	May Classic

Training Program

- **Easy:** 6-7 miles, but more runs were continuous than those of freshman year. Typical pace was in the low-7:00 range (7:00-7:20 per mile). Easy runs were the same pace as cross country, but did not consist of as many long runs.

- **Steady:** Same distances as easy. Either:
  - o start off easy and get progressively faster (i.e. 7:30 pace per mile, then work down to 6:20 per mile); or
  - o a few miles to warm-up, then about 4 miles steady at approximately 6:25 pace per mile, then 1-2 miles to cool-down.

- **Tempo:** Shorter distances than easy or steady, but: 1 mile warm-up, then 3 miles at 5:50-6:05 pace per mile, then a 1 mile cool-down. Sometimes, tempos would be split into 2 x 2mile instead.

- **Interval:**
  - o Ladder workout – with 2+ minutes in between each rep; sometimes took 2-3 minutes break midway through the workout
    - 400m in 1:09
    - 400m in 1:08
    - 800m in 2:25
    - 1200m in 3:48
    - 400m in 1:09
    - 400m in 1:08
  - o 800m Repeats – with 2-3 minutes recovery between each rep
    - 6x800m in 2:33, then 2:31, then 2:30, then 2:29, then 2:29, then 2:28
  - o 200m Repeats – with 2:00 recovery between each rep
    - 10x200m (ranging from 0:33-0:34 per rep)

Junior Cross Country – 2007

| Maximum Mileage: 59 |
| Average Mileage: 40 |

		Workouts							
Week	Miles	M	Tu	W	Th	F	Sa	Su	Race(s)
1	24	E	E	X	E	X	E	X	
2	35	E	S	E	E	X	E	X	
3	44	T	S	E	S	X	E	E	
4	52	T	S	E	S	X	S	E	
5	55	T	S	S	E	X	E	E	
6	59	T	S	E	X	E	S	E	
7	59	T	S	E	X	E	S	T	
8	56	E	E	S	T	S	X	E	
9	45	S	T	S	I	X	I	E	
10	43	S	T	E	I	X	E	I	
11	37	S	T	E	I	X	T	X	
12	39	S	T	E	E	R	E	X	Sunset
13	35	E	T	E	I	X	R	E	Red Mule
14	43	S	T	E	I	X	E	E	
15	44	S	T	E	I	X	R	E	LOL
16	36	S	I	X	R	E	X	E	Plant
17	38	T	E	E	I	X	R	E	Southern Stars
18	35	S	I	E	I	X	R	E	Flrunners
19	32	E	X	S	I	E	X	E	
20	41	T	X	R	S	S	T	E	County
21	40	S	I	X	R	E	T	E	Postal
22	31	T	I	E	R	X	S	E	Districts
23	35	T	I	E	X	R	E	S	Regions
24	22	T	E	I	E	X	R	X	State
25	30	E	S	E	R	X	S	X	Turkey Trot
26	32	I	E	S	X	E	R	X	Madd Dash
27	27	E	I	E	X	E	R	X	Bolt Run

Training Program

- **Easy:** 7-8 miles. Most runs were continuous. Once a week "long runs" of 11-12 miles during the summer base period. Pace was now in the mid-6:00 range.
- **Steady:** Same distances as easy. Either:
  - start off easy and get progressively faster (i.e. 7:05 pace per mile, then work down to 5:50 per mile); or
  - a few miles to warm-up, then about 4-5 miles steady at approximately 5:55 pace per mile, then 2 miles to cool-down.
- **Tempo:** Distances now the same as steady runs; no longer broken up; longer warm-up, then 3-4 miles at 5:40 pace per mile, then a cool down of 1-2 miles.
- **Interval:** Split times getting much faster; recovery times decreasing to under 1:00 between reps for shorter workouts, and no more than 2:00 between reps for longer workouts. Breaks midway through workouts still occurred, but were rare.
  - Descending Ladder Workout – with less than 2 minutes recovery time between reps:
    - 2x1200m in 3:45, then 3:42
    - 2x800m in 2:27, then 2:25
    - 2x400m in 1:08, then 1:07
  - 1600m Repeats – with less than 2 minutes recovery time between reps:
    - 3x1600m in 5:15, then 5:14, then 5:07
  - 1200m Repeats – with less than 2 minutes recovery time in between each rep:
    - 5x1200m in 3:59, then 3:58, then 3:56, then 3:53, then 3:49)
    - Also, finish the workout with some striders in the grass of about 50m each
  - 400m Repeats – with 1:30 recovery in between each rep:
    - 8x400m in 1:12, then 1:11, then 1:11, then 1:10, then 1:10, then 1:09, then 1:09, then 1:08)
    - Also, finish with 3x200m in 0:33, then 0:32, then 0:31

Junior Track – 2008

Maximum Mileage: 54
Average Mileage: 36

		Workouts							
Week	Miles	M	Tu	W	Th	F	Sa	Su	Race(s)
1	26	E	X	S	X	E	X	E	
2	44	E	T	E	T	E	S	X	
3	53	X	E	T	I	E	T	S	
4	54	X	T	E	I	S	E	S	
5									
6									
7									
8									
9									
10									
11	26	E	S	T	I	E	I	X	
12	28	I	E	R	E	X	I	E	Districts
13	32	I	S	X	R	E	I	T	Regions
14	21	E	I	T	E	X	R	X	State

Note: *Perhaps going from 0 to 26 to 44 to 53 miles of intense training over a very short period of time may be more conductive to injury than to outstanding performance. I know now that I won't repeat that workout routine in the future.*

Training Program

- **Easy:** 7-8 miles. Almost every run was continuous and had pick-ups towards the end. This was the first track season where I needed to mix in long runs during the weeks than I was racing. Pace was now in the mid-6:00 range (6:20-6:40 per mile).
- **Steady**: Same distances as easy. Either:
  - start off easy and get progressively faster (i.e. 7:05 pace per mile, then work down to 5:50 per mile); or
  - a few miles to warm-up, then about 4-5 miles steady at approximately 5:55 pace per mile, then 2 miles to cool-down.
- **Tempo:** Distances now the same as steady runs; no longer broken up; longer warm-up, then 3-4 miles at 5:30-5:45 pace per mile, then a cool down of 1-2 miles.
- **Interval:** Split times getting much faster; recovery times decreasing to under 1:00 between reps for shorter workouts, and no more than 2:00 between reps for longer workouts. Breaks midway through workouts still occurred, but were rare.
  - Alternating Distances Repetition Workout – with 1:00 recovery for the entire workout.
    - 3x200m in 0:32, then 0:31, then 0:30
    - 3x200m (all-out)
    - 400m in 1:10, then 800m in 2:30
    - 400m in 1:11, then 800m in 2:32
    - 400m in 1:09
  - 800m Repeats – with 0:45 recovery between each rep:
    - 8x800m (all between 2:36 and 2:41)

__Note__: During the 6 weeks that I was unable to run, I did plenty of cross training to stay in shape. I swam 5-6 days per week and made sure to simulate all of my running workouts (i.e. easy, steady, tempo, interval) while in the pool. Scott Sepessy taught me how to swim; my dad, a former collegiate swimmer, designed my workouts. Those workouts were lap swimming, NOT aqua-jogging. Here are some sample swim workouts (notice that they too progress in difficulty and length):

# of reps		Yards				Total Yards
1	x	400	Warm-up		=	400
			stretch -- shoulders and ankles			
8	x	50	on	1:00	=	400
6	x	50	on	:55	=	300
4	x	50	on	:50	=	200
1	x	50		easy	=	50
4	x	100	on	1:50	=	400
3	x	100	on	1:45	=	300
2	x	100	on	1:40	=	200
1	x	100		easy	=	100
8	x	50			=	400
1 length underwater; followed by 1 length easy swim; 30 seconds rest between each 50						
1	x	250	Cool-down		=	250
		Total Yards for Workout			***=***	***3000***

# of reps		Yards			Total Yards
1	x	400	Warm-up	=	400
			stretch -- shoulders and ankles		
8	x	50	"steady"; 10 sec rest	=	400
6	x	50	"tempo"; 10 sec rest	=	300
4	x	50	"race"; 10 sec rest	=	200
1	x	50	easy	=	50
6	x	100	"steady"; 10 sec rest	=	600
4	x	100	"tempo"; 10 sec rest	=	400
4	x	100	"race"; 10 sec rest	=	400
1	x	100	easy	=	100
8	x	50		=	400
1 length underwater; followed by 1 length easy swim; 30 seconds rest between each 50					
1	x	150	Cool-down	=	150
		Total Yards for Workout		***=***	***3400***

# of reps		Yards			Total Yards
1	x	500	Warm-up	=	500
			stretch -- shoulders and ankles		
1	x	400	"steady"; 10 sec rest	=	400
1	x	50	easy	=	50
3	x	300	"steady"; 10 sec rest	=	900
1	x	50	easy	=	50
5	x	200	"steady"; 10 sec rest	=	1000
1	x	50	easy	=	50
7	x	100	"steady"; 10 sec rest	=	700
1	x	50	easy	=	50
1	x	100	Cool-down	=	100
			Total Yards for Workout	**=**	***3800***

# of reps		Yards			Total Yards
1	x	150	Warm-up	=	150
			stretch -- shoulders and ankles		
1	x	500	"steady"; 10 sec rest	=	500
1	x	400	"steady"; 10 sec rest	=	400
1	x	300	"steady"; 10 sec rest	=	300
1	x	50	easy	=	50
2	x	300	"tempo"; 10 sec rest	=	600
2	x	250	"tempo"; 10 sec rest	=	500
2	x	200	"tempo"; 10 sec rest	=	400
2	x	150	"tempo"; 10 sec rest	=	300
2	x	100	"tempo"; 10 sec rest	=	200
1	x	50	easy	=	50
2	x	100	"race"; 10 sec rest	=	200
3	x	50	"race"; 10 sec rest	=	150
4	x	25	"race"; 10 sec rest	=	100
1	x	100	Cool-down	=	100
			Total Yards for Workout	**=**	***4000***

Senior Cross Country – 2008

Maximum Mileage: 66
Average Mileage: 47

		Workouts							
Week	Miles	M	Tu	W	Th	F	Sa	Su	Race(s)
1	18	E	X	E	X	E	E	X	
2	23	E	S	X	S	E	X	X	
3	26	E	E	X	E	X	S	E	
4	30	X	E	S	X	S	E	E	
5	36	S	E	E	S	X	E	S	
6	42	E	S	E	S	X	E	T	
7	48	X	S	E	S	T	E	S	
8	57	X	S	E	S	E	S	T	
9	62	E	E	T	E	S	X	E	
10	64	S	T	E	S	S	X	E	
11	66	T	E	I	S	E	X	E	
12	60	T	E	I	S	X	T	E	
13	61	T	E	I	S	X	R	E	Red Mule
14	64	T	E	I	S	X	E	S	
15	58	T	E	S	I	X	S	E	
16	60	T	E	I	S	X	R	E	UF
17	57	T	E	I	S	X	R	E	FSU
18	44	T	X	I	E	I	E	X	
19	50	I	E	I	X	E	S	E	
20	54	I	E	T	S	X	R	E	Pre-State
21	41	E	X	E	I	E	I	S	
22	45	X	R	E	T	E	S	E	County
23	38	T	S	X	R	E	T	E	Districts
24	37	S	I	E	E	R	E	X	Regions
25	37	S	I	E	E	X	R	E	State
26	38	E	I	S	E	E	R	X	NXN – S.E.

Training Program

- **Easy:** 8-9 miles. Tried to make every run continuous, after a short warm-up. Once a week "long runs" of 13-15 miles during the summer base period. Pace was now at sub-6:00 per mile.

- **Steady**: Same distances as easy. Either:
  o start off easy and get progressively faster (i.e. 6:50 pace per mile, then work down to 5:40 per mile); or
  o a few miles to warm-up, then about 5-6 miles steady at approximately 5:40 pace per mile, then 2 miles to cool-down. Striders were now on every-other day.

- **Tempo:** Distances continued to be the same as steady runs; pace dropped as well (5:20 pace per mile); longer cool downs afterwards (usually 2-3 miles).

- **Interval:** Split times getting much faster; recovery times were now vital; Integration of thresh-hold workouts to work on running "comfortably hard"; workouts were much longer, with shorter speed at the end of workouts. No more breaks midway through workouts.
  o "Fartlek" Workout – alternating interval/jogging workout, typically run on a golf course or hilly cross country course; continuous run for 6 miles total; repeat the 3:00, 2:00, 1:00 pattern for the entire run; the "fast" parts should feel like an effort close to interval pace.
    - 3:00 fast, then 2:00 jog
    - 2:00 fast, then 1:00 jog
    - 1:00 fast, then 0:30 jog
    - then, repeat until 4 miles is completed
  o Ladder Workout – with 1:30 recovery time between reps:
    - 4x200m in :33, then 0:32, then 0:31, then 0:30
    - 2x400m in 1:07, then 1:06
    - 3x1600m in 5:20, then 5:17, then 5:14
    - 4x200m in 0:31, then 0:30, then 0:29, then 0:28
  o 1600m Repeats – with less than 1 minute recovery time between reps:
    - 4x1600m in 5:02, then 4:58, then 4:56, then 4:54

Senior Track – 2009

Maximum Mileage: 55
Average Mileage: 40

		Workouts							
Week	Miles	M	Tu	W	Th	F	Sa	Su	Race(s)
1	18	E	X	E	X	X	E	X	
2	25	E	X	E	E	X	S	X	
3	29	E	X	E	S	S	X	E	
4	36	S	E	S	S	X	E	X	
5	43	S	E	I	I	E	X	S	
6	50	S	I	E	T	E	E	X	
7	54	S	I	E	R	X	E	E	Blue/White
8	20	S	E	X	X	X	E	E	
9	45	E	E	S	I	E	X	S	
10	34	I	E	R	E	R	E	X	JHS Tri; NIN
11	48	S	I	E	I	X	R	E	Bob Hayes
12	49	S	I	E	E	R	R	E	FSU (2 days)
13	50	T	I	E	X	R	R	E	UF (2 days)
14	48	I	E	I	E	X	R	E	UT
15	46	I	E	X	R	E	I	E	Districts
16	44	I	E	S	X	R	E	I	Regions
17	33	S	I	E	E	X	R	X	State

Training Program

- **Easy:** 8-9 miles. Tried to make every run continuous, after a short warm-up. "Long runs" still weekly, but not as long as cross country season (usually 10-12 miles), and stopped within a month of the State Championship. Pace was now at sub-6:00 per mile.
- **Steady**: Same distances as easy. Either:

- o   start off easy and get progressively faster (i.e. 6:50 pace per mile, then work down to 5:40 per mile); or
- o   a few miles to warm-up, then about 6 miles steady at approximately 5:40 pace per mile, then 2 miles to cool-down. Striders were on every day of steady running.
- **Tempo:**   Distances continued to be the same as steady runs; pace dropped as well (5:20 pace per mile); longer cool downs afterwards (usually 2-3 miles).   Tempo running mainly occurred at the beginning of the season, and then interval training took precedence.
- **Interval:** Split times now tried to simulate racing paces and were very difficult with such short recovery times; continued thresh-hold, but with even longer distances; <u>One key factor was running several 200m repeats (all sub-0:30) after speed workouts were completed.</u> Really worked on turnover this season in order to make my kick very strong.
  - o   Ladder Workout – with 100m jog recovery between reps:
    - 4x200m in 0:31, then 0:30, then 0:29, then 0:28
    - 2x300m in 0:46, then :047
    - 2x400m in 1:06, then 1:05
    - 2x800m in 2:18, then 2:15
    - 2x400m in 1:05, then 1:04
    - 2x200m in 0:30, then 0:29
  - o   Repeat Groups workout – with 100m jog recovery in between each rep, and 1:30 recovery time after each group set.   One example was 5 sets of 200m, 200m, 400m:
    - 200m in :33, then 200m in :32, then 400m in 1:08
    - 200m in :32, then 200m in :31, then 400m in 1:07
    - 200m in :31, then 200m in :30, then 400m in 1:06
    - 200m in :30, then 200m in :29, then 400m in 1:05
    - 200m in :29, then 200m in :28, then 400m in 1:04
  - o   1000m Repeats – with 0:45 recovery time between reps:
    - 10x1000m in 3:28, then 3:26, then 3:24, then 3:22, then 3:20, then 3:19, then 3:18 then 3:17, then 3:16, then 3:15

* * * * * * *

Recording YOUR Workouts

After figuring out what your training should be for the season, you should record every day's run in a running log. Many people buy running logs and prefer to hand-write the information, whereas other people prefer to make their own spreadsheets on a computer. Either way, the point is simple: write EVERYTHING down.

Throughout high school, I kept detailed DAILY records of my running activities. So, I would know EXACTLY, on a day-by-day basis:

- where I ran
- how far I ran
- what pace I ran
- how I felt before, during, and after I ran
- what cross training I did
- what I ate
- what seemed to be working and not working
- any thoughts about my run, my mood, my feelings, etc.

I also kept weekly and cumulative records of:

- mileage completed
- amount of mileage on each pair of running shoes
- weight
- shoe size

I wrote down random thoughts. I wrote down what was helping me and what was not helping me. I wrote down notes about my physical and mental states. I wrote down goals for each year and for my high school career as a whole, so that I could plan for my improvement throughout high school (of course, I will be doing the same thing for my college running). I wrote down EVERYTHING.

Here is a template to use for your own running log. I used a similar format, but my notes expanded well beyond the small box on the bottom and the margins on the side of the page.

Running Log					
Week # -- From __ / __ to __ / __					
Day	Location /Route	Type of Run	Workout Explanation	Notes	Mileage
MON.					
TUE.					
WED.					
THU.					
FRI.					
SAT.					
SUN.					
Weekly Notes:					

* * * * * * *

Recording YOUR Races

After evaluating each workout in a running log, you should make results spreadsheets. Making these charts will allow you to: evaluate how each race went during the season, compare how you raced to prior years, and track your progression through each season (i.e., racing faster as you approach the State Championship). In addition, since college coaches want to know how well you progress from season to season and during a specific season, this will be a great way to get a head start on your college selection process. I cannot over-emphasize how impressed college coaches were with how well organized I was when I presented my performance spreadsheets to them. They could easily track my progress and chart out how they could expect me to perform over the coming seasons. I am convinced that this process separated me from the countless other high school students that may have approached the same coaches. Obviously, if you are an All-American distance runner or a Footlocker finalist, your results will get the attention of the coaches, but for you or I, who started high school as average or above average runners, this process is what gives you a competitive edge. (I will give further details of my experience with the college recruiting process in Chapter 8.)

My own results spreadsheets from my senior cross country and track seasons are found in Appendix 3. But, here is a template that you can use to track your own race performances.

_____ _____'s Races – Current Season (Year)								
				PRs:				
					Course Comparisons			
Date	Race	Time 2009	Place	Race Type	SR	JR	SO	FR
Notes:								

Making Connections
The Recruiting Process

College Fair

On a sunny morning in October 2006, I remember coming to Tropicana Field in St. Petersburg for an annual college fair. An impressive display of college representative booths swarmed the turf, setting up a chaos amongst the sea of people. The most congested lines were at the popular in-state universities, such as the University of Florida, Florida State University, the University of Central Florida, and the University of South Florida. There were plenty of kids dressed in suits that approached the ivy-league kiosks, hoping to impress any admissions representative handing out pamphlets.

But my dad and I were alone at the handful of simply decorated booths – all information desks for small colleges that were virtually unknown to me. Those schools included Bowdoin, Swarthmore, Bates, Colby, Hamilton, and Colgate. I sighed, rolled my eyes, and slipped over to my dream school – Duke University. I even wore blue and white that day, hoping that the Duke alums would notice my dedication to this fine school. However, when I started to ask the admissions representative a question, I was promptly cut off by "Name. Email. Address. Have a nice day...Next!" '*How rude*,' I thought to myself. That was when I realized that I should have listened more closely to what those liberal arts schools had to offer. It didn't hit me until later: the college representative from Bowdoin's booth was a classmate of Joan Benoit Samuelson, the gold medalist of the inaugural Olympic women's marathon in 1984. I started to think that maybe those smaller schools had something to offer to me – they treat students like people, not just an insignificant number – and that I could offer something to them.

Starting to Excel

Since I'll be using my mind a lot longer than I'll be using my running speed, I focused on academics in my college search, with the hope that some of the outstanding colleges and universities would offer the proper mix of academics and athletics.

I also did some self-evaluation (see my resume in Appendix 1). I recognized that I was just average in terms of board scores, but was motivated enough to be ranked in the top 5-10% of my class at Jesuit High School. That was no small feat since it is an extremely competitive high school with lots of really bright students. In fact, half of our top runners managed a perfect score on one or more of the parts of the SATs; one of my classmates scored a 36 (perfect score) on the ACT; my classmates were accepted to such schools as Harvard, MIT, Cal Tech, Amherst, University of Chicago, Northwestern, University of Pennsylvania, Dartmouth, Cornell, etc. So, I treated my academics very much like I treated running – just like I was a guy with average foot speed that could compete with some of the fastest guys in the State, I felt that, given my average intellect, I could still compete academically, and even excel, with the top students around. I, therefore, set my goals to go to a top tier college or university and was confident that I had enough to offer a school to be an attractive candidate.

Of course there was one drawback in targeting these very selective schools – I would be eliminating any opportunity for an academic scholarship. Also, lots of smaller colleges compete at the Division III collegiate level, and do not give athletic scholarships.

Researching Schools

I then went through extensive research, using the internet and college guidebooks, analyzing the schools I had seen at the College Fair. I came across more colleges with strong academic and athletic recognition – including Middlebury, Amherst, and Williams. Most of those schools were located in the Northeast, and I felt that a significant change in weather and lifestyle could produce many more positive results with my running

To do as extensive a search as possible, I started with a few sources – such as princetonreview.com, collegeprowler.com, and usnews.com – that have lists and rankings of the top universities and colleges in the country, based on such items as:

- academics
- athletics
- quality of life
- housing
- dorms
- weather
- security
- transportation
- food (which is extremely important for distance runners like myself who can consume nearly 7,000 calories per day)

College Prowler Rankings

For example, collegeprowler.com was a great starting point, and I used that reference to note the following schools that received its highest grades in academics, based on: professors being knowledgeable, accessible, and genuinely interested in their students' welfare; class size; how well professors communicate; whether or not classes are engaging; etc. to the following universities and colleges (listed alphabetically):

Amherst	Emory	Scripps
Bard	Fashion Institute	Smith
Barnard	Georgetown	Stanford
Bates	Georgia Tech	Swarthmore
Bowdoin	Grinnell	Trinity
Brandeis	Hamilton	Tufts
Brown	Harvard	UC – Berkeley
Bryn Mawr	Harvey Mudd	UCLA
Cal Tech	Haverford	U of Chicago
Carleton	Johns Hopkins	U of Michigan
Carnegie Melon	Kenyon	U of Penn
Case Western	Lawrence	U of Rochester
Reserve	Macalester	USC (CA)
Claremont McKenna	McGill	U of Virginia
Clark	Middlebury	Vanderbilt
Colby	MIT	Vassar
Colgate	Northwestern	Washington & Lee
Colorado College	Notre Dame	Washington University
Columbia	Oberlin	Wellesley
Connecticut College	Pomona	Wesleyan
Cornell	Princeton	William & Mary
Dartmouth	Reed	Williams
Davidson	R. I. School of Design	Yale
Duke	Rice	

U.S. News Rankings

I also made extensive use of the U.S. News & World Reports Annual Rankings of top universities and colleges. Those rankings are somewhat comparable to the Princeton Review and College Prowler. They are broken down by:

- **Top national universities** – which are generally large, research-oriented universities, are characterized by undergraduate as well as graduate programs and typically have such programs such as business, engineering, medicine, law, etc.
- **Top liberal arts colleges** – which are typically smaller, private colleges, emphasize undergraduate education (most of them don't even have graduate programs) and award at least half of their degrees in the arts and sciences

Armed with the information from U.S. News & World Reports rankings, I began my formal search with its top 35 national universities (which included seven of the larger state universities – *in italics below*) and its top 25 liberal arts colleges, which are presented here in rank order:

Top National Universities

1. Harvard (MA)
2. Princeton (NJ)
3. Yale (CT)
4. MIT (MA)
4. Stanford (CA)
6. Cal Tech
6. U of Penn
8. Columbia (NY)
8. Duke (NC)
8. U of Chicago
11. Dartmouth (NH)
12. Northwestern (IL)
12. Washington U (MO)
14. Cornell (NY)
15. Johns Hopkins (MD)
16. Brown (RI)
17. Rice (TX)
18. Emory (GA)
18. Notre Dame (IN)
18. Vanderbilt (TN)
21. UC – Berkeley
22. Carnegie Mellon (PA)
23. Georgetown (DC)
23. U of Virginia
25. UCLA
26. U of Michigan
27. USC (CA)
28. Tufts (MA)
28. Wake Forest (NC)
30. UNC
31. Brandeis (MA)
32. William and Mary (VA)

33. NYU
34. Boston College
35. Georgia Tech

Top Liberal Arts Colleges

1. Amherst (MA)
1. Williams (MA)
3. Swarthmore (PA)
4. Wellesley (MA)
5. Middlebury (VT)
6. Bowdoin (ME)
6. Pomona (CA)
8. Carleton (MN)
9. Davidson (NC)
10. Haverford (PA)
11. Claremont McKenna (CA)
11. Vassar (NY)
13. Wesleyan (CT)
14. Grinnell (IA)
14. Harvey Mudd (CA)
14. U.S.M.A. -- Army (NY)
17. Washington & Lee (VA)
18. Colgate (NY)
18. Smith (MA)
20. Hamilton (NY)
20. Oberlin (OH)
22. U.S.N.A -- Navy (MD)
23. Bryn Mawr (PA)
23. Colby (ME)
25. Bates (ME)

Narrowing the Search

I still recognized that the schools on these lists are nearly impossible to gain acceptance – and as for academic scholarships, that would be completely out of the question. They routinely reject valedictorians, kids with perfect board scores, etc. and their acceptance rates are generally between 10-20% (out of an outstanding applicant pool). However, I felt that my story would be good enough to at least get their attention.

Now came the process of elimination for me -- All of the schools just listed are outstanding in academics so I couldn't eliminate any schools as being too weak academically. However, I did establish a few basic criteria to focus my search for the ideal university or college:

- Get out of the southeast, where it's too hot to train
- Focus on the Northeast – stay in the same time zone as my family
- Want to avoid downtown, large cities
- I'm not brilliant and I'm not a tech genius, so I can eliminate a few of those schools that are primarily focused on science & technology
- Eliminate all-women's colleges and, although it was once a thought, eliminate military academies
- Eliminate some of the schools that have weaker cross country/track programs

That narrowed down my initial search from about 60 schools to about 20. My narrowed down list included a few Ivy League schools and some outstanding small, private liberal arts colleges:

Top National Universities	Top Liberal Arts Colleges
8. Duke	1. Amherst
11. Dartmouth	1. Williams
14. Cornell	3. Swarthmore
16. Brown	5. Middlebury
23. U of Virginia	6. Bowdoin
28. Tufts	9. Davidson
28. Wake Forest	10. Haverford
30. UNC	13. Wesleyan
31. Brandeis	18. Colgate
32. William and Mary	20. Hamilton
	23. Colby
	25. Bates

Out of these schools:

- Academic scholarships would be nowhere to be found. The only way to get an academic scholarship would be to go to a university for which I would be "over-qualified," and I am too much of an "over-achiever" to want to do that

- Athletic scholarships – at least partial (which would mean perhaps a 1/8 share of a scholarship, if I'm lucky) MIGHT be available from a couple of the larger state universities on the list, and since I wanted a smaller school, those larger ones would not be at the top of my list. The remaining schools – i.e., the Ivies and the small liberal arts colleges – do not offer athletic scholarships. The only way to get an athletic scholarship would also be to go to a university for which I would be over-qualified and/or which was desperate for my running talents. However, being among the top runners on a collegiate team BEFORE I even start training with the school is definitely not the scenario I wanted.

So, I realized that college would be expensive for my family and for me. I would have to rely on their ability to pay for college and whatever I could contribute from money earned from my writing (this book, for example).

Visiting Schools

I now had a manageable list and could start the college tours in an efficient manner. My (unofficial) college visits began the summer after my sophomore year. Despite coming off a somewhat frustrating season, my times and my improvement thus far were good enough to get the attention of some coaches. Having broken 10:00 in the 3200m and 17:00 in the 5K as a sophomore really helped me, but, hopefully some coaches would see my potential to run below 9:30 and 16:00 in those distances over my next two years of high school.

Therefore, I worked through coaches, not admissions offices. I emailed a lengthy introduction about myself, with a resume and spreadsheet of my race results attached. I wanted to show I was different than the many people that just fill out a recruiting questionnaire and then get generic recruiting letters once a month. I wanted to have one-on-one communication with the coaches.

Most coaches were extremely responsive and I would say that about 80-90% were eager to meet me after my initial emails to them. A few never established a relationship, partly because I was not looking to pursue them. The result was that in two short college trips, I would be able to meet with the coaches, see the campuses, and narrow my options even further – and, hopefully, come up with my first, second, and third choices. Then, all that would be left would be to hope that the colleges that I loved would be the same ones that loved me just as much. So here were my two college touring trips:

Northeast/New England Trip

Top National Universities – 3 Ivy League schools in smaller cities

11. Dartmouth
14. Cornell
16. Brown

Top Liberal Arts Colleges – some outstanding small private colleges, mostly in small New England cities

1. Amherst
1. Williams
5. Middlebury
6. Bowdoin
18. Colgate
20. Hamilton
23. Colby
25. Bates

Atlantic Coast Trip – from North Carolina to Pennsylvania:

Top National Universities – a top tier private university and a couple of great state universities

8. Duke
23. *U of Virginia*
32. *William and Mary*

Top Liberal Arts Colleges – 3 outstanding small liberal arts colleges

3. Swarthmore
9. Davidson
10. Haverford

How I Spent My Summer Vacation

During one of my college trips with my dad, I had the opportunity to visit one of my highest choice schools. My dad was hesitant to even visit the school after receiving the Coach's short, abrupt email responses from prior weeks. Nonetheless, I hoped that the coach would be different in person than his emails suggested.

Unfortunately, the coach lived up to the arrogance of his emails, spending less than five minutes with me and constantly telling me that, "Division I is a whole new level than high school running. You have no idea what you would be getting into." It's true that I was not the most outstanding sophomore, but my 9:57 for 3200m at least showed potential. He still wasn't interested, even though I had three friends on the team (two of which were from my high school). He could care less about "hopeful drops in their times," however, since he wanted to see recruits be national-class very early on in their careers.

Ultimately, I ended up being faster than ALL of their recruits of that year by the time I was a senior, but by that time, I was no longer interested in that school.

That was a positive learning experience – it showed me the value of keeping my eyes open for new opportunities. In this case, what appeared to be a high choice turned out to not be a choice I should even consider. Lesson to everyone: keep your options open; what you may think is your dream school when you are in middle should not necessarily be the school that is a best fit for you.

A similar incident occurred at another university. When I came to the coach's office, he was extremely rude and said that he didn't have time to talk to me. I came all the way from Florida to visit a specific school and a coach said that I can't even talk to him? Thankfully, the assistant coach (who followed up with emails) was nice enough to give me some of his time, so I got to talk to him. But the important lesson is this – I became just as fast as their top recruits; the head coach just didn't have the patience to listen to my story about past and projected improvement. Apparently, he didn't put that much faith in Jack Daniels' VDOT levels and the improvement that is possible.

How College Coaches Can Make Your Day

Of course, there were other coaches who proved to be much more patient and encouraging of my situation. After all, I came to see them:

- showing a lot of interest in them, after having researched thoroughly their schools, their running programs, the performances of their teams over the last few seasons, the names of their assistant coaches and some of their runners, etc.;

- demonstrating how passionate I was about running and how determined I was to improve my performance by presenting them with detailed spreadsheets of my progress along with daily running logs;

- having just completed a somewhat successful sophomore year, and showing them charts of my progress – race by race -- over the past few years;

- being barely over 100 pounds and 5 feet tall and looking like a 12-year old, demonstrating that I could continue to improve as I got bigger and stronger and continued my dedication to the sport.

For example, I received great advice from the Dartmouth College Head Coach Barry Harwick. Dartmouth is a highly-regarded Division I school (both academically and athletically) – and Coach Harwick saw my progression early on in my high school career. Coach Harwick had planned out for me where I should be for my junior and senior years. I kept that advice in the back of my mind and not only did I make those marks, but I surpassed all of his and my expectations. He said that he wanted me to hit 9:35 in the 3200m by my senior year because that is where most of the recruits end up. He also emphasized steady progression – 9:45 by my junior year; 9:35 by my senior year. Then, he told me, "these are the three things that Dartmouth looks for in their student-athletes:"

(1) Academics
(2) Athletics
(3) Student really wants to attend (Translation: Dartmouth is #1 choice for college)

Similarly, Bates College Coach Al Fereshetian and Williams College Coach Pete Farwell both noticed my small physical stature as a sophomore and recognized the potential I had to improve in the future. Not only did they predict me being one of the elite runners in Florida by the time I would be a senior, but they also believed that I could be a National Championship contender at the collegiate level.

It is a great signal for eager recruits to have coaches who demonstrate that they could be "patient mentors." For example, the season packets that Coach Fereshetian of Bates gives to incoming freshmen focus on his long-term approach to distance running. He believes in at least an 8-10 year approach, as opposed to less than 4 years of impatience. This mindset has not only helped me improve throughout high school, but also has given me the confidence that I could make my mark the same way in college, if I train appropriately.

After my initial visits with coaches, I continued my constant communication with them, keeping them updated with my progress over my next two years in high school. I would send them my results spreadsheets from every race during my junior and senior years. Since I was continually improving, my story just got better and better to them.

Brotherly Love for Haverford

After visiting campuses and talking to the cross country coaches at several small schools, including Williams, Amherst, Bates, Bowdoin, and Middlebury, my interest sprouted with these quaint schools, all of which are Division III programs. I was now looking forward to an upcoming visit with Haverford College, another Division III program, which is located in suburban Philadelphia and has less than 1200 undergraduates.

I sensed that Haverford would provide a great balance of superb academics, outstanding cross country, and students that are similar in nature to myself – hard-working individuals who maximize their talents and want to improve the world. As soon as I stepped onto the Haverford campus, not only did I fall in love with this simple, quiet school, but I had the opportunity to meet the internationally recognized Coach Tom Donnelly. Unlike my previous 30-minute or 60-minute visits with college coaches, Tom spent over 3 hours talking to me about my aspirations and how I could fit in with Haverford's excellent cross country team. He showed me around the school and introduced me to students on campus, giving me the confidence that I would be comfortable at this overly-welcoming school. I stayed in touch with Tom religiously, writing him emails often about my continued progress: I would receive hand-written responses in the mail, which were of course more meaningful to me than a 1-line email response.

Tom had recognized my talents and potential almost immediately and could tell how much I could contribute to Haverford through athletics, academics, and many extra-curricular activities.

Haverford, and especially Coach Tom, noticed the "fine print" of my application. I came to the realization that Haverford looked at ALL aspects of an applicant. This school looked into the numbers and words on my resume to find the answers to the following: "Can we trust this person?", "Is he truly willing to improve society?", and "Will this student continue the tradition of a Haverford student, such as the upholding Honor Code, solving the world's toughest problems, and maintaining the intellectual and oratorical skills to positively influence the common man."

I went back to visit Haverford in the summer of 2008, where I not only gave Tom a pleasant surprise since I had grown about 5 inches and "bulked up" over my junior year, but I got to speak with him once again and had an interview with an admissions representative. I came extremely well-prepared and was glad that this interview, according to the interviewer, was a major factor in a student's application because it gave a voice to my resume and a personality to my application paperwork.

Division I vs. Division III

When I contacted Coach Tom Donnelly during the summer between my sophomore and junior years, he recognized several characteristics in me that he knew would be fitting for his already outstanding program. Tom saw my talent (whether it was explicit or implicit) early on and knew that I would have the potential to be an excellent collegiate athlete over the upcoming years.

Running for a Division I program is a perfect fit for some runners and those people probably shouldn't even consider looking at Division III program because they are already close to the caliber of professional athletes. However, I do feel that there are several high school runners in the country that are border-line DI/DII/DIII caliber – and sure enough most of them assume that DI is ALWAYS the better choice. Before I simply state "this isn't true," since you may think I'm biased towards going to a Division III program myself, please recognize that by my senior year, plenty of Division I schools were interested in me.

Several powerhouse Division I programs emphasize "the result" as opposed to "the process." Yes, they love numbers – but not hitting certain marks at certain times, in their opinion, means that a runner is simply not good enough. Some programs go as far to say, if you don't hit certain times by your junior year, then you simply cannot make the team. Last time I checked, there are four years in high school...not two or three. Many Division I coaches are caught up on their recruits' results early on in their careers, as opposed to the POTENTIAL for improvement, which is what I had going for me.

Decision Time

Once the first semester of my senior year began, I felt that I was ready to apply Early Decision to Haverford College. I was also extremely interested in Middlebury and Bowdoin and I also loved the environments and especially the coaches at Dartmouth, Williams, and Bates. There were great similarities among these six schools – specifically:

- small, top-tier liberal arts oriented programs generally located in college communities rather than large downtown cities; and

- cross country programs run by coaches with 25+ years of experience, who were highly regarded by their students and by other coaches.

Any one of those six outstanding schools would have been phenomenal for me – of course, there's also the matter of hoping that any of those schools would view me as worthy enough for their extremely selective standards.

Since I knew enough about Haverford already, I went on recruiting visits to both Middlebury and Bowdoin in the fall. Although the trips were fun and I would have been thrilled to spend the next 4 years working with either of the coaches – Coach Aldrich and Coach Slovenski -- I came to the conclusion that the environments were simply not the same as Haverford. Even though these three schools are very comparable academically, and offered a great quality of life and very good food, the students at Haverford seemed more focused with cross country training and had the uninterrupted determination to achieve greatness. This constant perseverance and the will to improve, in my opinion, would translate much better in the classroom for me. Plus, the cross country team, which came in 2nd place at the NCAA Division III Championship and was a perennial powerhouse, also won the National All-Academic Team of the year for both 2007 and 2008. This is an excellent indicator of how the students view their role in this world and how they feel obliged to improve it as much as possible.

Here is my Personal Essay that I submitted to Haverford College with my Common Application:

Haverford College Personal Essay

By: Jordan Schilit

I may not be the typical applicant at an institution as prestigious as Haverford. I have neither the natural brilliance, nor the near-perfect board scores that many candidates possess. Instead, I am an ordinary person with an inner fire who strives for goals that at one point may have seemed almost impossible. I truly believe in the philosophy that "heroes are ordinary people that have achieved extraordinary things in life."

Every day at Jesuit High School, I am surrounded by the brightest, the strongest, and the fastest – naturally gifted young men with the innate tools to have an enormous impact on the world. I attend a school which lives by its motto, "Men for Others," and has produced individuals who have achieved national prominence in business, the military, education, the ministry, and athletics.

Despite the fact that I entered JHS on a provisional acceptance and was required to attend summer school to prove that I could succeed at this school, I have set similarly lofty goals of impacting this world. JHS took a chance when accepting me. Yet, rather than judging me based solely on an entrance examination score, they recognized almost immediately my diligence, perseverance, and motivation. They were convinced that I belonged there and could contribute to the school and to the community, and could demonstrate what "Men for Others" represents. They have assured me that I have surpassed their initial expectations, through academics, athletics, and leadership. For example, I am ranked in the top 10% of my class while having taken a demanding schedule of honors and AP courses as well as college courses in the University of South Florida's Honors Program. I was elected president of the National Honor Society and have worked as Editor-in-Chief of the school literary magazine. I received awards for my artwork and earned an all-expense paid trip to Poland and Israel as a result of my award-winning essay on tolerance and the Holocaust. Athletically, I achieved All-State honors and was selected as team captain for cross country and track. Recently, I was named as one of only five recipients from the entire West Coast of Florida of the U.S. Military Academy's prestigious Schwarzkopf Award, presented annually to outstanding scholar/athlete/leaders.

To get the most out of one's limited talents is a virtue that will likely translate into superior long term success. That is a stark contrast to the individual labeled as "a waste of talent," who may have skipped studying because of his or her natural intelligence or may have missed practice because of his or her outstanding foot speed. According to former President Calvin Coolidge, "Nothing in this world can take the place of persistence. Talent will not; nothing is more common than unsuccessful people with talent. Genius will not; unrewarded genius is almost a proverb." Perhaps these gifted individuals never learned lessons in humility to enable them to be successful over a lifetime – and it's being successful over a lifetime, not just 2 or 3 years, that enables us to make our mark in this world.

Born with average intellect and decent athletic capabilities, I convinced myself early in my youth that my own success would result from motivation, sacrifice, diligence, and a burning desire to succeed, rather than from innate intellect and physical strength. I recognized that an ordinary person such as me can do extraordinary things, and that is what would define my "greatness." I've learned an important lesson in success from Senator Bill Bradley, who became a Hall of Fame basketball player, despite lacking the physique, speed, and jumping ability of his competitors. Senator Bradley's quote, "Ambition is the path to success. Persistence is the vehicle you arrive in." has shaped his life as an athlete, a politician, and as a humanitarian. As an athlete, I did not inherit the natural leg-speed of many high school runners; nevertheless, over 3 years, I gradually worked my way through the rankings from an average runner on my school team to an All-State competitor. College coaches keep telling me that this steady improvement is likely to result in great success as a college runner, in contrast to some of the naturally gifted runners who blossom at a young age and fall short of everyone's expectations.

My development as a distinguished student-athlete-leader will not stop at high school. At Haverford, I feel that I would get the foundation to achieve the lofty expectations that I have established for myself. As a student, I want to attend a high caliber liberal arts institution that is recognized internationally. As an athlete, my goals are to be part of a team's national championship, and to be recognized as both an All-American and Academic All-American runner. As a leader, I have lived my life adhering to such values as honor, individual dignity, tolerance, awareness of the greater good, and contributing to society; I want to be a model representative of the college for these values. At Haverford, I feel that I will find the perfect balance and the opportunity to reach and possibly exceed all of these goals.

I am grateful that I am forced to work hard every day of my life. I am forced to think about every math problem that I tackle and every lap that I run. It is this drive that enables me to excel and to get the most out of my studies, my athletics, and my school and community involvement. I often think of Confucius' insightful words, "Our greatest glory is not in never falling, but in rising every time we fall." I am an ordinary person, but I always set my sights on accomplishing the extraordinary.

Accepted

One of the high points of my senior year in high school was on December 15th, 2008 when I was accepted Early Decision to Haverford College. I was proud of that since Haverford is such a highly selective college – I have a friend who was the salutatorian of his school and had 1600 board scores, but was rejected from Haverford (however, accepted by Stanford) a couple of years ago. I knew I had sent my application to the best place for me in the country, since this institution noticed the numerous outstanding accomplishments I had achieved over the past four years, despite limited talents and abilities – "I am an ordinary person with an inner fire who strives for goals that at one point may have seemed almost impossible," as stated in my Personal Essay for Haverford College. With less than 1200 students in its student body, Haverford analyzes every possible aspect of an applicant's application and also the "unseen character" of the student.

I was thrilled to receive my acceptance to Haverford in December of my senior year, coming after a very strong cross country season. The media took note of my college decision, as demonstrated in Bob Cooke's article in flrunners.com:

Flrunners.com

Published: December 31, 2009

Smaller is Better, Schilit Commits to Haverford

By: Bob Cooke – ubjammin2@aol.com

Sometimes smaller is better; truly better if you're a "Ford" under the tutelage of one of the greatest Track and Field distance coaches the United States has ever known.

Tampa Jesuit harrier Jordan Schilit is one of those fortunate hard-working but not immensely talented distance runners who will shortly train under the watchful eye of a Coach with 62 regional and conference championships during a tenured career that started 34 years ago and shows no sign of abating. His future Coach's resume reflects credit for 113 All-American athletes of whom 24 ultimately became NCAA champions. This Coach knows how to "mold teams of decent but not exceptional high school athletes into elite college runners."

No, Jordan isn't being reincarnated into past lore and heading to Fayetteville to run for the now retired John McDonnell at Arkansas, but instead to Division III Haverford College to train and compete for another Coach of Irish descent and lineage whom many have called the "Greatest of Coaches; Coach Tom Donnelly and his "Fords of Haverford".

With a student body the size of some High School senior classes, Haverford's 1,169 students are a rare combination of diminutive excellence both athletically and academically. They are so well known academically, that US News and World Report ranks Haverford 10th in the nation for small colleges who matriculate at least 50% of their students with degrees in Liberal Arts field of studies.

The academic prowess of the distance runners at Haverford especially in recent times simply can't be matched. Coach Donnelly's Men's cross country team has been honored as National All-Academic Team recipients 2 years "running" and will be looking to 3-peat next season.

Consider these other academic and athletic accolades from the 2007-2008 season:

Men's outdoor track & field team won its 16th straight Centennial Conference title.

Women's outdoor track & field team claimed its third-straight Centennial Conference Championship.

Men's indoor track & field won its 14th Centennial Conference title in 15 years.

Men's cross country won its 15th consecutive Centennial Conference Championship and placed second at NCAA Division III Championships.

Women's indoor track & field won its third consecutive Centennial Conference Championship and fourth in the last five years.

For Jordan, being accepted to attend Haverford is a dream come true and he states, "he is thrilled to now be part of this excellent tradition." As cross-country Captain, first team All-State, President of the Tigers National Honor Society, a member of the schools Spanish and Social Studies Honor Societies, and editor-in-chief of "Lyre", the schools highly acclaimed annual literary publication, Jordan should fit right in at Haverford and continue furthering Haverford's values of individual dignity, academic strength, and tolerance. The fact he gets to run for Coach Donnelly is truly icing on the cake and for those of you attending the FACA Clinic this week, seek out Coach Marcus O'Sullivan of Villanova and bend his ear on just how fortunate he was to have Coach Donnelly in his corner as Coach and mentor over the years.

Coach Donnelly is so fascinating and his impact on generations of "Fords" so immense, that the New York Times felt compelled to write a feature article on his legacy as a Cross-Country and Track and Field Coach and teacher, that it's easy to see the reason why Haverford was Jordo's first choice for college.

With Jesuit's motto being "Men for others" and adhering to such values as honor, individual dignity, tolerance, awareness of the greater good, and contributing to society; sometimes smaller is better if it provides the "perfect balance and opportunity to reach and possibly exceed all of these goals."

It will be interesting to follow Jordan's accomplishments at Haverford over the next few years and hopefully with a little luck of the Irish and some good old-fashioned hard work he will be well on his way to his stated goal; to be part of a team's national championship, and to be recognized as both an All-American and Academic All-American runner.

http://fl.milesplit.us/articles/21265

What a great way to begin my winter break – I was all set for college, while the vast majority of my graduating class at Jesuit would be stressing out over their college choices for the next several months.

Going to the College of YOUR Choice

Here are some conclusions that I drew from an article that provides a great dialogue on the college recruiting process, featuring two coach experts – Coach Alan Versaw and Coach Jay Johnson. Excerpts from the article can be found in Appendix 4.

- Track/cross country recruiting is not like the major sports in college – i.e., football, basketball, and baseball
- There are three potential ways to get money from a college or university:
  - **Athletics:** Here is how the math works out. There are a very limited number of scholarships available for track/cross country athletes – a maximum of 18.0 per school for women and 12.6 per school for men in Division 1, and then 12.6 per school for both men and women in Division II. (There could be fewer scholarships available if a school is NOT fully funded.) That's for the entire team for their entire stay at the university. Assuming that the typical athlete could be in school for approximately 5 years (he or she is often red-shirted for a year in the better quality Division I athletic programs), then that comes out to 2-3 total scholarship offers for the incoming class for the entire men's track & field and cross country teams COMBINED (which means that the best of the best of the best athletes from these programs may be fortunate enough to earn a one-half or a one-quarter or a one-eight share of a scholarship, based strictly on athletic skill). How good do you have to be to get part of that scholarship pool? At the highest tier (athletically) Division I schools such as Oregon, Colorado, Wisconsin, etc., the Nike All Americans – i.e., those running 1:52 for 800m, 4:08 for 1600m 9:00 for 3200m and 15:10 for 5000m – will partake of SOME athletic scholarship money. Having slightly slower times will not shut out a candidate from athletic scholarship money; it will simply necessitate that a candidate would only expect to get a PARTIAL athletic scholarship at a lower tier athletic program.

o **Academics:** Having perfect board scores at Stanford means that a student may very well be at the bottom half of his or her class at such a prestigious university. At Stanford, the typical distance runner recruit is in the low 15's (that's in minutes) in the 5K and the high 15's (that is high 1500s) in the SAT. So, with outstanding academic credentials, it would be far more likely to get an athletic scholarship at a university that is at a slightly lower tier than Stanford.

o **Need:** The Ivies (which are Division I) and the top tier liberal arts colleges such as Amherst, Williams, Haverford, Middlebury, Bowdoin etc. (which are generally Division III) do not award athletic or academic scholarships. Therefore, the only scholarship money is based on need.

- Unfortunately, for MOST runners, especially those runners that do well academically (let's say 1200-1400 SAT scores) and are gifted athletically (let's say 9:30 for 3200m; 15:40 for 5000m), they often have the choice of attractive scholarship offers for schools that don't interest them or small (or 0% -- i.e., walk-on) offers at academically prestigious schools. The good news is that, at least those top schools are interested in them, which would not otherwise have been the case if they did not have such success on the track.

- Top tier Division I running programs make sense for some runners – perhaps for the Foot Locker finalists or the NIN or NON All Americans or for the high school runner who can break 4:10 in the 1600m or break 9:10 in the 3200m or break 15:15 in the 5000m. However, if you're not one of the top 100 distance runners in the country, then you may be in for a surprise. A 9:20-9:25 3200m runner (like myself), while certainly fast, is in the position of either being a second tier recruit or a walk-on at a high quality Division I program (which isn't so bad – at least the school MIGHT have a place for you that otherwise would not be available). That means he needs to train with the team, run 100 miles a week, expect to be red-shirted, and his chance may come when someone else, who has been over-training, gets that inevitable injury. That scenario may be appealing to some, but not to others. The alternative is to seek out either a lesser quality Division I program, where you can make a meaningful contribution or a Division II or Division III program, where you can certainly make a difference. As a 9:22 3200m/15:33 5000m runner, I was in the worst situation or the best situation. I was not quite fast enough to be a top tier recruit at a top tier Division I program, although several of these programs had some interest in me. However, I was an extremely attractive candidate for just about any other school. In choosing a high quality Division III program like Haverford, I'll be in a position to contribute to the school immediately.

- Although there's not a whole lot that you can do about this, the data suggests that the situation is far easier for girls than it is for boys (the message is that girls should take advantage of the situation and guys should put their energy into making themselves competitive on more than one dimension). As Coach Johnson noted, out of the top 50 finishers in a boys state cross country meet, 48 typically want to go on and run in college, but out of the top 50 finishers in a girls state cross country meet, only 10 want to go on and run in college. The implication is that an expression of interest in running by the 50th-place girl at a state cross country meet is likely to grab a college coach's attention far more quickly than an expression of interest from the 20th-place boy.

- Coaches can certainly give advice on the recruiting process and perhaps make an introductory phone call, but once the process begins, it is really up to the student athlete. The student must be proactive in the process; college coaches typically only contact candidates who have expressed an interest in the college first.

Where Now?
My Two Cents

Conclusion

When Head Coach Mike Boza was still at Jesuit High School, he came up with an acronym for the team rules: W.I.N.N.E.R.S. The letter I would like to emphasize is "I," which stood for the phrase: "Improvement is essential." Recently, I wrote a feature article for *Marathon & Beyond* magazine entitled – "Change: The Progression We Need." I thought I would end this book with some thoughts gathered from a combination of that article and an evaluation of my high school running career.

Steve Prefontaine was commonly quoted saying, "'You're too small, Pre.' 'You're not fast enough, Pre.' 'Give up your foolish dream, Steve.' But they forgot something, I have to win." At one point in his life, Steve Prefontaine actually was not fast enough. In fact, Pre may have even been considered nothing out of the ordinary early on in his high school career, failing to break: 2 minutes in the ½ mile, 5 minutes in the mile, and 10 minutes in the 2-mile during his freshman year. Ultimately, Pre became a legend in long distance running. However, besides his legacy as one of the most dominant runners in US history, Pre accomplished perhaps an extraordinary feat – from age 15 to 24 he improved every year in every distance he raced. Whether or not Pre was "*ever* fast enough," thinking about it never slowed him down.

In addition, I was fortunate enough to recently interview Ryan Hall (American Record holder in the ½ marathon). After speaking to him, I realized how privileged the running world is to have such an outstanding role model in Ryan Hall, who teaches us lessons in patience, persistence, and humility, each of which is a part of the life of a distance runner. As Hall told me, "Everyone on the starting line [at the Olympics] dreamed of winning, but only one won – but this is not important – the journey was what was important. Dream big, but let your dreams inspire how you live today. Dreams should not be about the end goal, but rather about day to day living." Hall claims that, although it may be nice to have American records or possibly a world record, "It's not all about me. I want to leave a legacy with my running, hoping that there will be future young Americans that will surpass my records and propel American distance running to the next caliber." Hall hopes that these young stars will have the confidence to run with the highest caliber runners, will be willing to fail, and will never give up until they have achieved greatness.

Every young distance runner can learn some valuable lessons from Pre and from Ryan Hall. I use Pre's improvement throughout high school and college to demonstrate that you do not have to be the fastest freshman on your team to reach All-American status in high school, and you do not have to be a national champion in high school to win an NCAA national title. Like Pre, I started off my running career relatively unnoticed. My freshman high school PRs were actually fairly close to his. Yet, my high school career has been filled with "near misses," which can either bring out the worst in a runner (i.e. frustration, quitting, etc.) or, as was in my case, can bring out the best in a runner (i.e. the desire to work harder and improve). As an 18:15 5Ker, I failed to make the Varsity A squad of my high school's state championship cross country team and was not included on the All-County roster as a freshman. Despite improving to a 17:30 5Ker, I missed second-team All-County as a sophomore. While still improving to a 16:30 5Ker, I missed First Team All-County as a junior. Despite further improving to a 15:33 PR in the 5K, I missed All-American status as a senior. And, despite winning a State Championship in the 4x800m relay, I have never won a team overall State Championship nor an individual State

Championship. Furthermore, despite working my way up through the rankings during my four competitive years of running, I spent my high school career over-shadowed by of one of my teammates, who was a national age group record holder and an All-American. Similar to Pre, I have used the constant "public reminders" of me not being fast enough as motivation to make a name for myself and to prove that, beginning next year when I enter collegiate competition at Haverford College, I have the potential to be among the nation's elite.

I use Hall's ability to connect with up and coming runners as the motivation to succeed and to, ultimately, be a role model for them. For Hall, the transition to the marathon was not only for his own benefit, but rather for setting the stage for USA distance running. Certainly, that has had an impact on my training, my persistence, my goals, and hopefully, on my success. As I transition to my college years during the upcoming fall, I hope to follow in the footsteps of Steve Prefontaine and Ryan Hall by moving up in the distances and continuing to improve as my body matures. I look forward to transitioning from the 5K to the 8K in cross country and from the 3200m to the 5K/10K in track.

I understand that I, like most successful high school runners, am currently not the fastest high school runner in the country. I also understand that I, like any other high school runner, can achieve steady, yet extraordinary improvements over every year of high school. That improvement has enabled me to qualify for Nike Indoor Nationals and to finish within a few seconds of All-American status. Similar to when Steve Prefontaine and Ryan Hall were children, I have set my sights on the Olympic Trials and, hopefully, the Olympics. That will only be possible if I continue to improve in the same way I have over my high school career. Perhaps, ultimately, I will be the one to start a running revolution of my own in the future, knowing that the torch will be passed to the next young distance star able to represent his country in the years to come.

Appendices

Appendix 1:
Resume

Jordan Michael Schilit

Highlights:

o *Honor student (graduated Summa Cum Laude)*
o *President of National Honor Society*
o *Editor-in-Chief of 3 school publications*
o *All-State athlete in Cross Country and in Track & Field; Nationally ranked performance at Nike Indoor Nationals (PR of 15:33 in 5000m); State Champion for 4x800m Relay (7:47, US #6)*
o *Recipient of Schwarzkopf Leadership Award (sponsored by U.S. Military Academy), presented to 5 outstanding high school scholar-athlete-leaders throughout the West Coast of Florida*
o *School's representative as top scholar-athlete for the Wendy's National High School Heisman Scholarship*
o *Representative of the USA at the 17th World Maccabiah Games in Israel in 2005 as a Junior athlete*
o *Recipient of an all-expense paid trip to travel to Poland and Israel for the "March of the Living" in a regional essay contest about the relevance of Elie Wiesel's memoir Night to today's society*
o *Contributor to several nationally recognized running publications*
o *Winner, "Best of Show" & "Best Senior AP Portfolio" at JHS Art Show*

Education: Jesuit High School (JHS); Tampa, FL; Class of 2009
GPA: 4.11
Haverford College; Haverford, PA; Class of 2013

Intended Major: interested in: Art & Design, Photojournalism, and English Composition
Intended Career: undecided

College Goals: (1) achieving excellence in a high caliber academic institution that is recognized internationally; (2) being successful in balancing the rigorous demands of academics, athletics, and leadership at that college; (3) gaining the necessary oral and written communications skills to succeed in my subsequent career and to have an impact on the world; (4) being recognized as an All-American and Academic All-American runner; and (5) winning an individual as well as a team NCAA cross country or track national championship by my senior year in college.

High School Academic Honors:

Freshman Year	*Sophomore Year*	*Junior Year*	*Senior Year*
Won "March of the Living" Essay contest	Inducted into Hispanic National Honor Society (inducted during Sophomore year while taking Junior level course)	General H. Norman Schwarzkopf Leadership Award (selected from high schools throughout Florida's West Coast)	Jesuit High School's representative as top scholar-athlete for the Wendy's National High School Heisman Scholarship
Principal's Honor Roll	Honor Roll	Honor Roll	Honor Roll
	The Lyre Award – Assistant Editor	The Lyre Award – Editor in Chief	The Lyre Award – Editor in Chief
		Elected President of National Honor Society	President of National Honor Society
		Art show awards (1st place in charcoal; 2nd place in gesture drawing)	Art show Awards ("Best of Show" 2009 and 1st place Senior AP portfolio)

High School Courses Taken *(AP and Honors Noted)*:

Freshman Year	*Sophomore Year*	*Junior Year**	*Senior Year*
English I	*Honors English II*	*AP English III -- Lang & Comp*	*Honors English IV*
Spanish II	*Honors Spanish III*	*AP Spanish IV*	Writing for Publication
Algebra I	*Honors Geometry*	*Honors Algebra II/ Trigonometry*	*AP Calculus*
Global Studies	*Honors World History*	*Honors American History*	*Honors American Gov't & Economics*
Integrated Phys Science	*Honors Biology*	Chemistry	
Speech	Art	*Honors Art*	*AP Art*
Biblical Literature	Church History	Ethics & Social Justice	Christian Life
Phys Ed			

In addition, during my Junior Year, I enrolled in 2 college-level courses (a total of 6 credits) on "The Holocaust and European History," through the University of South Florida Honors College.

Employment:

Freshman Year: approximately 50 hours throughout year	Sophomore Year: approximately 50 hours throughout year	Junior Year: approximately 50 hours throughout year	Senior Year: approximately 200 hours throughout year
			Milesplit.us — writing internship
			Flrunners.com (a milesplit.us affiliate) — writing internship
			flotrack.org — writing internship
			"Marathon and Beyond" magazine — feature article
			freelance writer
tutoring in Hebrew and Bar Mitzvah studies	tutoring in Math, English, and Hebrew		tutoring in Math, English, and Spanish
house sitting	house sitting	house sitting	house sitting
baby sitting	baby sitting	baby sitting	baby sitting

I've worked for the past several years because I find enjoyment in these jobs and I feel it gives me a greater sense of responsibility and appreciation of finances. As far as tutoring in Hebrew, it has given me a chance to maintain my Jewish identity while at a Catholic school.

Clubs/Activities:

Freshman Year	Sophomore Year	Junior Year	Senior Year
Lyre: Freshman Editor	*Lyre:* Sophomore Editor	*Lyre* (JHS literary publication): Editor-in-chief	*Lyre* (JHS literary publication): Editor-in-chief
		Editorial Staff, Yearbook	Editorial Staff, Yearbook
		NHS; elected President for Senior Year	NHS: President
	Spanish National Honor Society	Spanish National Honor Society	Spanish National Honor Society
		Rho Kappa (Honor Society for Social Studies)	Rho Kappa (Honor Society for Social Studies)
			Newspaper staff (Editor –in-chief and Contributor)
		Peer Ministry	Peer Ministry

As president of the National Honor Society, I have shown that I am capable of leading the most intelligent, athletic, and well-rounded seniors at JHS. Also, my editorial positions with The Lyre have been particularly important because they demonstrate my writing skills as well as my organizational capabilities. I had the opportunity to work with some of the best writers at JHS in putting together some excellent publications under significant time constraints.

Community Service:

Freshman Year:	Sophomore Year:	Junior Year:	Senior Year:
21 hours	20 hours	50 hours	80 hours
Metropolitan Ministries		Special Olympics	God's Pedal Power Ministry
Egypt Lake Elementary	Egypt Lake Elementary	Egypt Lake Elementary	Egypt Lake Elementary
United Synagogue Youth (USY)		Hearthstone Assisted Living	JHS Peer Ministry Team
Jewish Community Center (JCC)	Jewish Community Center (JCC)	St. Peter Claver Catholic School	S.O.A.R. Tutoring Program
Congregation Rodeph Shalom	Congregation Rodeph Shalom	Weinberg Village Assisted Living	Metropolitan Ministries

These activities were all rewarding. The projects in which I participated ranged from assisting the elderly, the needy, and the youth. My service at Egypt Lake was quite memorable because I have had the opportunity to use my skills in Spanish to assist Spanish-speaking students with their reading comprehension. In addition, I started a service project at Jesuit where seniors from the National Honor Society tutor freshman who are struggling in Spanish, Biology, Math, and English. I also found working at God's Pedal Power Ministry, a volunteer organization that repairs and donates bicycles to the needy, to have an extreme impact on the community.

Sports:

Cross Country
(15:44 PR in the 5K)

Freshman Year	*Sophomore Year*	*Junior Year*	*Senior Year*
		Team Captain	Team Captain
Member, State Champion team			Member, State Runner-Up team
			All-State
	All-County (Honorable Mention)	All-County (1st team)	All-County (1st team)
			ESPN RISE magazine Florida All-Area selection
		15th place - State	7th place - State
	5th place - Regions	4th place - Regions	Regional Runner-Up
		District Runner-Up	District Champion
	#3 or #4 runner on JHS team in most meets	#2 runner on JHS team in every meet	#1 or #2 runner on JHS team in every meet
			Member of State Runner-Up All-Academic Team

Track

(15:33 PR in the indoor 5000m, 9:22 PR in the 3200m, 4:22 PR in the 1600m, 1:58 PR in the 800m)

Freshman Year	*Sophomore Year*	*Junior Year*	*Senior Year*
		Team Captain	Team Captain, MVP Award
Member, State Runner-Up Team			Member, State Runner-Up Team
		All State (1st Team) – 3200m	All-State (1st Team) - 4x800m, 1600m, 3200m
		All-County	All-County (1st Team)
			Top-10 Nationally Ranked 4x800m team, school record holder
			ESPN RISE magazine Florida All-Area selection
			16th Place Nationally - Nike Indoor Nationals (5000m)
		6th Place - State (3200m)	STATE CHAMPION (4x800m), STATE RUNNER-UP (1600m, 3200m)
		4th Place - Regions (3200m)	Regional Champion (3200m); Regional Runner-Up (1600m, 4x800m)
8th place – Districts (3200m)	6th place - Districts (3200)	3rd place - Districts (3200m)	District Champion (3200m, 4x800m); District Runner-Up (1600m)

In addition, I represented the United States at the 17th World Maccabiah Games in Israel in 2005, a quadrennial Olympic-style athletic competition for Jewish athletes from more than 60 countries around the world.

Most admirable trait:

I am extremely well-rounded, balancing a few hours of cross country or track practice every day with my rigorous coursework. I strive for perfection in all my activities and go the "extra mile" with my studies and my running. The General H. Norman Schwarzkopf Leadership Award, sponsored by the U.S. Military Academy, which is presented to outstanding high school scholar-athlete-leaders, demonstrates my success in these areas. The selection process was as follows: First, I was selected as the Jesuit High School Class of 2009 representative. Then, I was one of 5 Schwarzkopf award winners for the entire West Coast of Florida.

Most significant academic accomplishment:

I received an all-expense paid trip to travel to Poland and Israel for the "March of the Living" in a regional essay contest about Elie Wiesel's memoir <u>Night</u> and its relevance to today's society. This trip brought together Jewish teens from all over the world (http://www.motl.org/programs/highSchool.htm). It began in Poland on Yom Hashoah (Holocaust Remembrance Day), where the participants marched from Auschwitz to Birkenau, the largest Nazi concentration camp complex, retracing the actual route that countless people were forced to take on their way to the gas chambers at Birkenau, and culminated in a trip to Israel in honor of Yom Ha'Atzmaut (Israel Independence Day – *Israel turned 60 this year*). Participants who have gone on this mission in previous years are forever overcome with emotion as they experience firsthand the stark contrast between the most tragic and the most joyful events in the history of the Jewish people.

Most significant non-academic accomplishments:

Before the start of my freshman year of high school, I was selected to represent the United States at the 17th World Maccabiah Games in Israel in 2005. I finished in the top ten for the Junior Division 1500 meter run, even though I competed against mainly high school seniors and college students. It was an accomplishment to compete at such a high-caliber competition at such a young age, being the youngest member on the entire U.S. squad. I am honored to have followed in the footsteps of some famous sports legends such as Mark Spitz and Lenny Krayzelberg (swimming), Kerri Strug (gymnastics), Brad Gilbert (tennis), and Dolph Schayes and Ernie Grunfeld (basketball), who have represented the United States at the Maccabiah games.

During my senior year, I finished my high school running career with the goals that I had hoped for as a freshman. I led the cross country team to a State Runner-Up team performance that had a team average fast enough to win any prior year in Florida history. I not only was team captain of the best cross country team in school history, but also led the Jesuit Track & Field team to a State Runner-Up team performance in 2009. I won a State Championship on the 4x800m relay team, which ran 7:47 – a new school record and 6th fastest in the USA for 2009. Also, instead of dropping out of the 1600m for an attempted 3200m title, my State Runner-Up finishes in the 1600m and 3200m gave Jesuit High School enough points to place 2nd overall as a team in the State Championship.

Hobbies/interests:

There are three interests that I've had that stand out: (1) running, which has provided me with the discipline and dedication to be successful in athletics and academics; (2) drawing/designing, which has given me a unique balance of creativity and discipline; and (3) writing, which has enabled me to communicate my interests to a large audience.

Publications:

"Interview with Ryan Hall," *flrunners.com*, February 2009
 (*Also appeared in* Milesplit.us *and* Tennessee Runner)
 http://fl.milesplit.us/articles/22026
 http://www.milesplit.us/articles/archive/2009/2
 http://tn.milesplit.us/updates/article_22026
"Ryan Hall: Heart of Lightness," *flrunners.com*, March 2009
 (*Excerpt also appeared in* letsrun.com *and* flotrack.org)
 http://fl.milesplit.us/articles/22115
 http://www.letsrun.com/2009/weekthatwas0316.php
 http://www.flotrack.org/articles/view/952-ryan-hall-heart-of-
  lightness
"Seven Tampa Runners Run Sub-2 800 Meters," *flrunners.com*, March 2009
 http://fl.milesplit.us/articles/22232
"Knights of the Banked Table: West Windsor-Plainsboro No. Seizes HSR @ 4
x 1Mile," *nj.milesplit.us*, March 2009
 (*Also appeared in* flotrack.org)
  http://nj.milesplit.us/articles/22268
 http://www.flotrack.org/articles/view/954-knights-of-the-
  banked-table-west-windsor-plainsboro-no-seizes-hsr-4-x-
  1mile
"Jordan Hasay: A Mission Transcending High School Running," *milesplit.us*,
April 2009
 (Also appeared in flotrack.org)
 http://www.milesplit.us/articles/22688
 http://www.flotrack.org/articles/view/946-jordan-hasay-a-
  mission-transcending-high-school-running
"Sickles' Wehunt Vying for Strong Finish," *flotrack.org*, May 2009
 http://www.flotrack.org/articles/view/1137-sickles-wehunt-
  vying-for-strong-finish
"From Sub-par to State Shocker: Sickles' 4x8 Relay Blazes to Best in Florida,"
flotrack.org, May 2009
 http://www.flotrack.org/articles/view/1152-from-sub-par-to-
  state-shocker-sickles-4x8-relay-blazes-to-best-in-florida
"Redefining the PR: Thompson Valley's Perfect Relay," *flotrack.org*, May 2009
 http://www.flotrack.org/articles/view/1153-redefining-the-pr-
  thompson-valley-highs-perfect-relay

Contact information:
Jordan Michael Schilit
813-601-RUNR (813-601-7867) - cell
http://www.freewebs.com/jordo1010/
jordan@schilit.net

Appendix 2:
List of Race Performances

Here is a list of all of my elite performances on flrunners.com (http://fl.milesplit.us/athletes/27794):

Note: This list does not include:

- Freshman Year and most of Sophomore Year, when I did not have any elite performances
- Relay splits

Also, note: PR= personal record; SB= season's best

5000 Meter Run
(Cross Country, unless noted otherwise; RR = road race)

08-26-06	17:00.00	SB	Red Mule 5K **(RR)**
10-25-06	16:55.90	SB	Al Lopez Open Cross Country 5K Race
11-03-06	17:09.00		FHSAA 2A Region 3
04-20-07	16:17.00		Spartan Sprint 7 **(RR, short course)**
05-05-07	16:33.00		GunnAllen Financial May Classic **(RR)**
08-24-07	16:52.00		Southern Stars Sunset 5K
09-01-07	16:23.56		Red Mule Runners Labor Day Run
09-15-07	16:39.00		Land O Lakes Gator Invitational
09-29-07	16:14.00		Southern Stars Invitational
10-05-07	16:42.83		flrunners.com Invitational 8
10-17-07	16:35.00		Hillsborough County Championship
11-01-07	16:12.00	SB	FHSAA 2A District 5
11-09-07	16:59.02		FHSAA 2A Region 3
11-17-07	16:44.00		FHSAA CC State Finals
11-22-07	16:30.00		Times Turkey Trot **(RR)**
12-01-07	16:04.00	SB	MADD Dash for SADD (Lap 6) **(RR)**
12-08-07	16:26.00		Tampa Bay Lightning Reindeer Run **(RR)**
08-30-08	15:47.00	SB	Red Mule Run **(RR)**
09-20-08	16:36.46		UF Mountain Dew CC Invitational

09-27-08	16:07.43	<u>FSU Invitational</u>
10-18-08	16:09.08	<u>Little Everglades Pre-State Invitational</u>
10-28-08	15:56.00	<u>Hillsborough County XC Championship</u>
11-06-08	16:08.00	<u>FHSAA 2A District 5</u>
11-14-08	16:36.27	<u>FHSAA 2A Region 3</u>
11-22-08	15:55.00	<u>FHSAA CC State Finals</u>
11-29-08	16:06.00	<u>Nike Cross Nationals Southeast Regional</u>
12-06-08	16:26.42	<u>FACA All-Star Meet</u>
03-13-09	15:33.23 PR	<u>Nike Indoor Nationals</u> **(Indoor Track)**

3200 Meter Run (Outdoor Track)

03-24-07	9:57.50 SB	<u>UT Distance Carnival</u>
10-25-07	9:45.00 SB	<u>Two Mile Postal</u>
04-09-08	9:59.55	<u>FHSAA 2A District 9</u>
04-17-08	9:56.07	<u>FHSAA 2A Region 3</u>
04-25-08	9:50.19 SB	<u>FHSAA 1A-2A Outdoor State Finals</u>
03-20-09	9:44.25	<u>Bob Hayes Invitational</u>
03-27-09	9:31.68	<u>FSU Relays</u>
04-11-09	9:22.30 PR	<u>UT Distance Carnival</u>
04-16-09	9:45.56	<u>FHSAA 2A District 9</u>
04-24-09	9:42.21	<u>FHSAA 2A Region 3</u>
05-02-09	9:43.27	<u>FHSAA 2A State Finals</u>

1600 Meter Run (Outdoor Track)

04-03-09	4:24.45	<u>Florida Relays</u>
04-16-09	4:31.10	<u>FHSAA 2A District 9</u>
04-24-09	4:23.02	<u>FHSAA 2A Region 3</u>
05-02-09	4:22.89 PR	<u>FHSAA 2A State Finals</u>

800 Meter Run (Outdoor Track)

03-11-09	1:59.50 PR	<u>Jesuit/AHN, Sickles, Robinson</u>
03-11-09	2:03.17	<u>FSU Relays</u>

Appendix 3:
Charting My Results

Here are some examples of how you could fill out your own race results spreadsheets. These are all from my senior cross country and track seasons:

Cross Country 2008

Jordan Schilit's Races (5K) - 2008								
				PRs:	15:44	16:04	16:55	17:32
					Course Comparisons			
Date	Race	Time 2009	Place	Race Type	SR	JR	SO	FR
8/30	Red Mule 5K	15:47	3rd	Reg. - wide	15:47	16:24	17:00	17:32
Notes:	Fast course; nice conditions. Raced against some of the top-ranked individuals in the state. I ran a very smart and evenly-paced race, cutting nearly 40 seconds off my previous best on this course and bettering my PR by 17 seconds. My mile splits were: 5:00, 5:10, 5:00. No team scores.							
9/20	UF Gator Invite	16:36	9th	State - wide	16:36	n/a	17:43	n/a
Notes:	Slow course; very hot day. The race started at 9:40 am as opposed to the usual 8:00 am start time. The times were about 20 seconds slower than everyone's PR. The winner won with a 15:57, but ran 15:38 at the Red Mule 5K. Despite cutting over 1:00 off my previous best on this course, this was a mediocre race performance. The race was run on UF's hilly golf course and requires many surges to run well, unlike my common "smooth and progressive" running strategy. I was the 4th place runner for 2A. Jesuit High School placed 2nd overall behind defending 2A State Champion Belen Jesuit.							
9/27	FSU Invite	16:07	6th	State - wide	16:07	n/a	17:34	18:34
Notes:	Good course (fair amounts of uphills and downhills); nice conditions -- weather was in the 70s during race time. Raced against some of the top-ranked runners in the state. I placed 6th, only behind runners ranked either #1 or #2 for their respective classifications. Our #1 runner at Jesuit ran 15:51 (PR is 15:38) and placed 2nd, but was only 15 seconds in front of me. I came through the 2-mile at 10:31, so my last mile was under 5:00. My time on this course (16:07) was about a 1:30 improvement from my last race here as a sophomore. Jesuit High School placed 1st.							

10/18	Pre-State Meet	**16:09**	16th	State-wide	**16:09**	16:43	18:05	18:11
Notes:	Nice weather; fair course. This is one of the more challenging courses in Florida, but the competition included ALL of the best teams and individuals from around the State, so the times were generally fast. I made some tactical mistakes early on in the race, going out very fast (4:53) and not being able to hold on. I faded from an early top-5 placing to eventually out of the top-15. Relative to more local competition, I was less than 20 seconds behind our #1 runner and finished as the 6th place 2A finisher (a good indicator of where I stand right now for the State Championship). Jesuit High School was 5th overall and was the 3rd place 2A team.							
10/28	County Champ.	**15:56**	4th	County-wide	**15:56**	16:35	n/a	n/a
Notes:	Great weather (in the 50s); nice course. I ran a very smart race, starting out in 8th place for the 1st mile, moving up to 6th in the 2nd mile, and then finishing up with a strong kick for 4th place overall. I beat Jesuit's #1 runner (who has 4:14, 9:17, and 15:38 credentials) for the first time in my high school career. I was 20 seconds back from the leader (15:36), who has a PR of 15:25 and is ranked 2nd for 4A. However, I was only 5 seconds off of the second place finisher -- who has a PR of 15:38 and is ranked 3rd for 3A. I cut almost 40 seconds off my time from last year, and closed the gap or beat many of the Florida's top runners. Jesuit High School placed 1st and was named County Champion.							
11/3	District Champ.	**16:08**	1st	Dist. - wide (2A)	**16:08**	16:12	16:55	17:49
Notes:	Hot day, but ran on a good course. I ran this race very conservatively at the beginning and moved up progressively towards the second half of the race. I passed our usual #1 runner at about 2.5 miles, and finished over 20 seconds ahead of the 2nd place finisher. The course was a bit longer than last year (15 seconds because of an extra turnaround), but nevertheless I still ran faster. This was my 1st District Individual Championship of my high school career. Jesuit High School placed 1st and was named District Champion for the 11th consecutive year.							
11/14	Regional Champ.	**16:36**	2nd	Reg. - wide (2A)	**16:36**	16:59	n/a	n/a
Notes:	Very hot and humid day; extremely tough course. This course had a plethora of hairpin turns and consisted of uneven footing and sand along the entire course. Also, the temperature was in the mid-80s and very muggy, whereas last year was much nicer weather -- in the low-60s. I ran the beginning of the race very conservatively, starting out at 7th place for mile 1 and 5th place at mile 2. At about 2.2, I moved up into 2nd place and held on for the remainder of the race. I went through the 2-mile at 10:45 and finished up with a 5:15 last mile, finishing only 10 seconds off the leader (Jesuit's usual #1 runner). Placing 10 seconds behind the leader (ranked #2 in 2A), I finished ahead of the #3 ranked individual for 2A, who has a PR of 15:40. Jesuit High School placed 1st and was named Region Champion.							
11/22	State Champ.	**15:55**	7th	State-wide (2A)	**15:55**	16:44	18:02	18:13

Notes:	Very nice weather; same course as the Pre-State meet. I ran the entire race with our team's usual #1 runner, until he out-kicked me at the finish to come in 3 seconds in front of me. I went out at 5:00 for the mile and passed runners along the entire course; I was not even in the top-20 runners until the 1.5 mile mark, and then worked my way up to 7th by the last quarter-mile. I ran this race very smartly, but may have been able to break the top-5 if I wasn't as conservative at the beginning of the race. The team had a 23-second 1-5 spread, averaging 16:06. Jesuit High School placed 2nd and was named State Runner-Up.							
11/29	NXN -- S.E.	**16:06**	34th	S.E. USA - wide	**16:06**	n/a	n/a	n/a
Notes:	Cold conditions; challenging course. This North Carolina course has what Dyestat.com calls "the hill that never ends," which runners have to climb twice during the course. This race started off very fast because of the steep downhills, so I came through the mile at 4:45. By the end of the race, I was completely spent and had zero energy left for any kick once I climbed that massive hill. I finished the race just over 16:00, but felt I could have been closer to sub-15:50 if I had more left at the end of the race. Jesuit High School did not qualify for Nike Team Nationals, but was able to beat Belen Jesuit -- the team that beat us last week for the 2A State Championship							
12/2	5000m Time Trial	**15:44**	1st	School - wide	**15:44**	n/a	n/a	n/a
Notes:	Cool temperature, but very windy. I ran the first 1.5 miles with our other lead runner, but he dropped out at the 3200m mark. Therefore, I had to run about half of the race on my own, but still managed to record a lifetime best. This is my first time running a 5000m race on the track and I have not been training for track-type races; therefore, my time should improve significantly in the 5K at Nike Indoor Nationals.							

Track 2009

Jordan Schilit's Indoor 5000m Race - 2009								
				PRs:	15:33			
					Course Comparisons			
Date	Race	Time 2009	Place	Race Type	SR	JR	SO	FR
3/13	Nike Indoor Nationals	15:33	16th	Nat'l Champ. Race	15:33	n/a	n/a	n/a
Notes:	This was one of my best race performances thus far, since I recorded a huge PR in the 5K and raced well, despite racing indoors for the first time. I started this race very aggressively, passing the 1st mile in 4:46 and then the 2nd mile in 9:46. I wanted to go out very hard in this race and see if I could hold on to a faster pace, since I did not want to feel like I had more energy left once I finished (i.e. the State Championship for XC was way too conservative). I was determined to run a big PR tonight, since I came all the way up to Boston for a National Championship race and I am still looking for that breakthrough performance. I finished in 16th place overall out of 29 runners; I was 5 seconds away from 12th place and 16 seconds away from All-American (top-6).							

Jordan Schilit's Outdoor 3200m Races - 2009								
				PRs:	9:22	9:50	9:57	10:39
					Course Comparisons			
Date	Race	Time 2009	Place	Race Type	SR	JR	SO	FR
3/21	Bob Hayes Invite	9:44	1st	State-wide	9:44	n/a	n/a	n/a
Notes:	Cool temperatures, but VERY windy. I managed to run a 1-second PR for 3200m even with 30mph winds during the entire race. It was so windy that 2 seconds taken off per lap would be a reasonable comparison to more runner-friendly conditions (thus a 9:28 effort would have been very realistic today). I led the first mile, splitting 4:47 and then finished very strong (1:07 last lap) for a 4:57 second mile. Four of the runners I beat have placed in the top-5 for their respective cross country classifications and were running faster than me during cross country season. My time of 9:44, even though I faced tougher conditions, was 4 seconds faster than last year's winner (Michael Wallace). Last year, Wallace ran 9:48 at Bob Hayes, then ran 9:22 at the FSU Invite, and then went on to win the State Championship in 9:25. Also, Guillermo Echarte was 2nd at Bob Hayes with 9:48, then ran 9:25 at the FSU Invite, and then came in 2nd at the State Championship with 9:29. This was a very strong race performance and ranks among the best of this season.							

3/27	FSU Relays	**9:31**	9th	State-wide	**9:31**	n/a	10:07	n/a
Notes:	Cool temperatures, but VERY rainy and windy. I went out with the lead pack for the 1st mile, splitting 4:41 (about 6 seconds back from the leader). I got gapped from the 8th place runner at about 5 1/2 laps, causing me to do most of the work on my own for the end of the race. I managed to run a 1:06 last lap to finish the 2nd mile in 4:50. I ran a PR in the 3200m tonight with my 9:31 effort, placing 9th in one of the deepest and fastest fields of 3200m runners in FL history. This was a very strong performance in my opinion, but I still feel that I have some room for improvement as I approach the State Championship series.								
4/11	UT Distance Carnival	**9:22**	1st	State - wide	**9:22**	n/a	9:57	10:39
Notes:	PERFECT conditions; excellent weather. I had the fastest seed-time (9:31 going into this race, and clearly showed my dominance over the field, winning by 15 seconds. I went out in 2:20 for the first 800m, but ran a 66-second third lap and then continued to increase my lead with a 4:35 first mile. I had easily separated the rest of the field at this point and was all alone for my 4:47 second mile. I ran a new PR of 9:22 and believe that this was one of my best race performances, since I was so smooth the entire race and had to do all of the work on my own. I was extremely confident in this race, and must have this same mindset and strategy in order to win the 2A State Championship. My 9:22 moves me up to #2 for 2A this year.								
4/16	District Champ.	**9:45**	1st	Dist. - wide (2A)	**9:45**	9:59	10:14	10:51
Notes:	Cool temperatures, very good conditions. This was my third race of the day, but I still managed to run 14 seconds faster than last year (even though I was fresh last year). I went out conservatively (4:51) and ran pretty close to even splits for the second mile (4:54). I put on a slight surge to make sure I had a secure lead, but ran very comfortably other than that. I beat 2nd place by 13 seconds.								
4/24	Regional Champ.	**9:42**	1st	Reg. - wide (2A)	**9:42**	9:56	n/a	n/a
Notes:	Cool temperatures, but poor air quality (forest fires nearby). It was a bit easier to breathe than earlier in the day, but this was also my third race of the day. I started off very conservatively, crossing the first mile in 4:55. I came back during the second mile very smoothly finishing with a 4:47 split and still felt very fresh. I made sure to make laps 5 and 6 my fastest splits, but I just cruised other than that for most of the race. I was surprised at how easy it felt to run just over 9:40 and furthermore doing this all alone. I feel I will be prepared for an extremely fast time next week, since I will be dropping out of the mile beforehand on May 2nd.								
5/2	State Champ.	**9:43**	2nd	State-wide (2A)	**9:43**	9:50	n/a	n/a
Notes:	Cool temperatures, nice weather. This race went out slow from the beginning (4:54), but I did manage to pick up the pace in the 2nd mile (4:49). However, I was pretty spent from my previous two races, so I								

was really only trying to hold on to 2nd place. I finished strong and cut the lead much closer from what is was during lap 6, but I just wanted to hold on to 2nd place (I didn't want to die and score less than 8 points). This concluded an awesome State Championship meet, since I accounted for 26 points. I still came home with 4 medals and my first State Title.

Jordan Schilit's Outdoor 1600m Races - 2009								
				PRs:	**4:22**	**n/a**	**4:46**	**4:59**
					Course Comparisons			
Date	**Race**	**Time 2009**	**Place**	**Race Type**	**SR**	**JR**	**SO**	**FR**
2/19	Jesuit Home Meet	4:33	2nd	School-wide	4:33	n/a	n/a	5:02
Notes:	Warm conditions, since race was in early afternoon. I had some hip pain this week (and during the race), but I still managed to run a PR in the 1600m, finishing 16 seconds behind my #1 miler (who has a PR of 4:14). I did not feel comfortable during this race and it was difficult getting into a smooth rhythm, but this can be seen as a good sign because of: (1) my lack of experience in the mile, and (2) shows that there is much room for improvement.							
4/3	UF Relays	4:24	11th	State-wide	4:24	n/a	n/a	n/a
Notes:	Cool temperatures, nice conditions. I ran this race in the 2nd heat because I only had one 1600m performance to enter, giving me a disadvantage in that I would have to do most of the work in this section. Nonetheless I managed to beat a few of the runners in the fast section, winning my heat in 4:24 -- a new PR. I had a very strong last 200m, passing 2 people over that stretch and then winning by over 3 seconds. My last 400m was 65 seconds. I feel that I have a very good shot at breaking 4:20 if I am fresh and am in a faster heat this year.							
4/16	District Champ.	4:31	2nd	Dist. - wide (2A)	4:31	n/a	n/a	n/a
Notes:	Cool temperatures, nice conditions. This race was very tactical and was a slow pace for me, since I was pacing our #3 runner to advance to the Regional Championship. I was in the back of the pack (about 10th place) for the first 800m and then moved up to 2nd place by the start of the 4th lap, crossing 1200m in 3:31. I had a very strong kick (60 second last 400m), finishing only 1 second behind our #1 miler (4:11 PR). My splits were 72, 70, 69, 60.							
4/24	Regional Champ.	4:23	2nd	Reg. - wide (2A)	4:23	n/a	n/a	n/a
Notes:	Moderate temperatures and very poor air quality (forest fires nearby). I was once again told to pace our #3 miler, so I went out very conservatively in this race, passing the 1200m mark in 3:24. I tried to help him keep up along the way, but by the 1200m mark he had faded way back, so I picked it up significantly for the last 400m, running a 59-							

	second last lap. I was surprised that I managed to PR since the air quality was so bad and that I also had in mind my 3200m race would start in less than an hour.							
5/2	State Champ.	**4:22**	2nd	State-wide (2A)	**4:22**	n/a	n/a	n/a
Notes:	Cool temperatures, nice weather. First, I did not even know for sure that I would be running the 1600m at the State Championship, since I had planned to run a fresh 3200m. However, the #2 seed dropped out for that same reason, so I felt I could pull-off a 2nd place finish with Connor in the lead. Sure enough, Connor and I had our 1-2 finish in the race -- a first in Jesuit HS history. This race was extremely tactical, since my splits were: 65, 75, 64, 58. Connor and I hung in the pack, trying to save energy for our later races, so as we started the bell lap -- I tapped him on the shoulder and we blasted the last 400m. I finished 3 seconds in front of 3rd place (who was last year's State Champion in the 3200m). Connor finished only 1 second in front of me. My 2nd place finish was the difference-maker for the team finishing 2nd overall at the State Championship.							

Jordan Schilit's Outdoor 800m Races - 2009								
				PRs:	1:59	n/a	n/a	2:20
					Course Comparisons			
Date	**Race**	**Time 2009**	**Place**	**Race Type**	**SR**	**JR**	**SO**	**FR**
3/11	Jesuit Tri-Meet	**1:59**	6th	School-wide Tri-meet	**1:59**	n/a	n/a	2:20
Notes:	Perfect weather, cool evening. I had not run this event since freshman year, but nonetheless managed to go under the 2:00 barrier. I went out in: 57 for the first 400m, and then put on a very strong kick in the last 100m to finish in 1:59.50. I finished as the 3rd-fastest JHS 800m runner this evening and was 6th place overall. The winner was 1:52 and 3 school records were set in this race. This was a breakthrough race because I came through for JHS when the team did not necessarily think I could break 2:00; thus, giving them confidence that I can contribute to a State-Championship defending 4x800m team.							
3/27	FSU Relays	**2:03**	17th	State-wide	**2:03**	n/a	n/a	n/a
Notes:	Very humid and windy (the track was still drenched from last night's thunderstorms). This was not a very strong performance by me, since some people from the slow heat managed to run faster than I did. I crossed the first 400m in 59 and then had very little energy for any kick in the second lap. I will put this race behind me and know that I have more chances to run fast 800m times in the 4x8 relay.							

Date	Race	Split Time	Team Place	Race Type	Team Total Time
3/21	Bob Hayes Invite	2:02	2nd	State-wide	8:17
Notes:	Cool conditions; windy, but not nearly as windy as the 3200m today. I anchored this relay, running the second-fastest leg (2:02) for my team. I received the baton very far behind the first place team (with a 1:52-PR anchor) and very far in front of the 3rd place team; thus, I know I will run faster during an earlier leg because I will have people to compete against. My time was solid, but I know I should be running either 2:00 or sub-2:00 during a 4x800m, since the team is going after the school record of 7:54.				
4/16	District Champ.	2:00	1st	Dist.-wide (2A)	8:02
Notes:	Very hot weather (middle of the day). I ran the 3rd leg of this 4x8 in a split on par with our fastest runner today (1:59). My splits were 59, 61 -- a solid effort considering the scorching weather and the fast that we ran on an asphalt track. Also, I had to run this split all alone, since we had a commanding lead by this point.				
4/24	Regional Champ.	1:58	2nd	Reg.-wide (2A)	8:02
Notes:	VERY HOT weather, terrible conditions (forest fires nearby). It was extremely difficult to breathe during this race because of all of the smoke flying around in the air. Nonetheless, I ran the fastest split for the team today (1:58), even though I had the 3rd fastest PR. I helped increase the lead significantly, but after the 3rd and 4th legs (2:04 and 2:00), we ended up coming in 2nd as a team by a ½ second. My splits were 58, 60. I figure that I can run closer to the 1:56 range, based off of this effort in such miserable conditions.				
5/2	State Champ.	1:58	1st	State-wide (2A)	7:47
Notes:	VERY HOT weather, but the air quality was much better this week. I tied my PR this week (1:58), running the 3rd leg of our STATE CHAMPIONSHIP winning 4x800m team. The team split 1:57, 1:57, 1:58, and 1:55, running 7:47 -- a new school record by 7 seconds. This time is currently ranked #6 in the USA. It was neat to see that the first 3 legs of the relay all ran faster than their times from March 11th, where conditions were perfect and we could only hope for a sub-7:50 effort. This reality came true on May 2nd because it was a total team effort at the 2009 2A State Championship.				

Table title: Jordan Schilit's Outdoor 4x800m Relay Races - 2009

Appendix 4:
Excerpts from Alan Versaw/
Jay Johnson Dialogue

Colorado Track XC
Published: February-March, 2008

College Recruiting: A Give and Take, Part I - Introductions
By Alan Versaw; February 18, 2008 (http://co,,milesplit.us/articles/21864)

In this feature, coaches Jay Johnson and Alan Versaw exchange information and perspectives on the college track and field/cross country recruiting process.

From this point forward, Coach Versaw's words will be printed in plain text. Coach Johnson's words will be printed in italicized text, making it easy to discern the voice you are hearing.

* * * * *

Over the nine years that I have been coaching high school distance runners, I have listened to a handful of college coaches speak to athletes and high school coaches about the recruiting process. While some of what I have learned from those sessions has proven helpful, there have also been some serious disconnects between what I heard and what I see happening in practice.

With an eye toward sharing some ideas I had to make this whole process less aggravating and more efficient, I started a conversation with Jay Johnson. Jay formerly handled recruiting at the University of Colorado and was partially responsible for bringing former Buffs Stephen Pifer and Brent Vaughn to CU. Jay has left, at least for the time being, the college recruiting scene, but remains actively involved in coaching high-level distance runners. You can spy on him at www.coachjayjohnson.com.

I ran into Alan Versaw, girls and boys coach at The Classical Academy, last week at a local coaching clinic, which was a nice reminder that I first meet him four years ago at a local coaching clinic. Alan shared with me that he was frustrated in regard to the college track and field/cross country recruiting process. Now, at this juncture, it's fair to ask, "Why does Alan Versaw's opinion matter?" or "Who the hell is he and where does he get off criticizing a fellow group of coaches?" Fair question and I submit two replies:

1) His girls team qualified for Nike Cross Nationals this fall.

2) He's the Colorado editor of co.MileSplit.us; while all HS coaches do a great job of knowing who the best runners in the state are, Alan's analysis culminates in an interesting dénouement each year when writes the "Class of 2009 College Choices" article for co.MileSplit.us.

So Alan and I are going to do something simple over the coming weeks. He's going to share an observation/frustration/anecdote about the recruiting process from the HS coaching perspective; I will share the counter-argument/position/frustration from the college coach's perspective. Though I'm no longer a college coach, the assumption is that I know what I'm talking about, having recruited at both the JUCO and NCAA Division I levels... and, yes, assuming that I know what I'm talking about is indeed a sizable assumption.

*   *   *   *   *

College Recruiting: A Give and Take, Part II - Scholarships
By Alan Versaw; February 19, 2008 (http://co,,milesplit.us/articles/21885)

The starting point of any discussion here has to be the number of available scholarships: 18.0 per school for women and 12.6 per school for men in Division 1, and then 12.6 per school for both men and women in Division II. I don't know if NAIA has any similar limitations on numbers.

It shouldn't take a very perceptive individual to understand that this mandates some serious spreading of the frosting. We all hear about the occasional full-ride student-athlete, but when you divide the available scholarships by five—according to the number of years most student-athletes take to use up their NCAA eligibility, you realize schools have maybe four full scholarships (or equivalent) to award for women and a little over two for men with each incoming class. And that assumes that the school in question is fully funded! Many schools, especially many Division II schools, are not fully funded, meaning they have fewer—often far fewer—than the maximum number of scholarships available to offer.

I try to do a good job of explaining to my athletes not to expect much. Honestly, I have to tell most of our guys not to expect anything, and to be delighted if they are offered anything beyond an invitation to walk on. Of course, I've never coached anyone who could chase down German Fernandez. But, frankly, a very large number of high school coaches don't know or haven't really thought over the implications of the numbers I just talked about. Equally as many high school coaches prefer not to be involved in the process and leave parents and athletes more or less on their own. And, ultimately, it isn't the job of the high school coach to break down the arithmetic of the available scholarships for the college coach.

Okay, here's the deal – you probably don't know a male distance runner who has received a full ride scholarship to an NCAA DI school that annually makes the NCAA championships. Why? Well, at the Stanfords, the Oregons and Arkansas's of the world, a boy who runs 1:54, 4:06 and 8:55 for 800m, 1,600m and 3,200m will definitely be recruited, but he won't get a "full grant-in-aid," i.e. the "full ride" that everyone talks about. My guess would be that he'd get roughly 50% athletic money at those three schools, so for the remainder of this comparison we'll say all three schools are offering this young man 50% (Note: This is just my best guess – DO NOT call up these programs when an athlete runs 1:53.9, 4:05.9 and 8:54.9 and ask for "the 50% scholarship Jay talked about.").

Now let's assume he has 34 on the ACT. Great – he'll likely get some academic money at Arkansas and maybe some at Oregon, but Stanford? Not a chance; it's Stanford and when you walk into a class of 30 kids on that campus and you have 34 on your ACT you'll be in the bottom fiftieth percentile of ACT scores.

I don't want to go into too much detail here, but I can safely say that the most frustrating thing during my years recruiting at CU was not being able to offer any academic money to kids who had 35 on the ACT or 1560 on the old SAT. I hated watching other hard-working coaches (Louis Quintana at Arizona State is the first that comes to mind) give that 35/1560 kid at least 50% academic money and sometimes up to 70%. That allows that same coach to offer only 30%-50% athletic money - the same amount that we were comfortable offering - for the kid to tell the local paper that he is going to school on a "full ride." Did that coach want the athlete more than we did? No. But parents, athletes, and HS coaches often equate the amount of money being offered with "how much they want Johnny," when the reality is that the schools in question, at least when it comes to athletic money, want him equally because they're each offering 50% grant-in-aid.

We could go on and on - and we will in the coming weeks – about what you have to run to expect X amount of athletic money, but let me explain what coaches mean when they say 50% grant-in-aid. Each institution comes up with a dollar figure, a figure that includes tuition, fees, room and board, books and usually a small allowance for personal expenses (clothes, travel, etc.). Most schools will call this the "cost of attendance" and state schools will have a different number for their in-state students vs. their out-of-state students: here are CU-Boulder's current numbers. So if you attend Lincoln HS in Denver and are offered a 50% scholarship then it's worth about $11,630 (half of the $23,261 – the on campus housing number since you'll live on campus as a freshman at CU).

There are numerous questions you should have at this point and I'll let you ask them in the comments section, but let me make something clear – I always hated the idea that Johnny is "worth $11,630" because he can run 1:54/4:06/8:55. Putting a number, a metric, on a person just felt wrong to me, yet I was fairly adept at "getting kids" for 20% when the other DI offers ranged from 50% to 100%. As I write this I can see the faces of two young men who turned down "fulls" at other places to come to CU for 20% - both won Big 12 titles in their respective fortés, both competed at the NCAA outdoor championships, and both had their scholarships increased throughout their careers as they ran faster. Not every school "bumps" you up when you run faster, but I can proudly say that Mark Wetmore bumped me from a walk-on to a scholarship athlete in 1995. He does it every year with athletes who deserve it. So even though the system does place a metric on a HS athlete, it's not inherently amoral or wrong, especially when the end of the story is a great education, great teammates, and big PRs.

*   *   *   *   *

College Recruiting: A Give and Take, Part III - Scholarships
By Alan Versaw; February 21, 2008 (http://co,,,milesplit.us/articles/21894)

Most students who have good grades and who have run fast have an interesting continuum of options by the middle of their senior year; big scholarship offers from schools they're not interested (yep, that sucks) and small offers or 0%, i.e. walk-on offers, at academically prestigious schools (yep, you want that education but the offer is small).

What to do as a family? Be honest about how important the scholarship is and have a candid family meeting about it. In my family it was simple - I wanted to walk on at CU, turning down the DII offer that would have paid 80% (I forget the athletic and academic breakdown - I had good, not great, test scores and was a 4:30 kid at the time - decent, but not great). My parents said that we could afford CU, provided I work each summer to earn any and all money needed for my super cool, super trusty 1979 Ford F150 truck (two-wheel, not four-wheel, drive, but still very cool...arguably the only reason my wife initially dated me). I was quite nervous having that conversation with my parents, but it was a conversation that needed to happen. If you're a family that cannot afford to send your son or daughter to a school that costs $40,000 a year, yet your son or daughter will get 80% of their education paid for at a school that costs $16,000 a year, then you need to explain to your son or daughter how important the scholarship money is. The flip side is that many students don't need the money and the scholarship becomes an ego issue for - in rank order - dad, HS coach, mom... with my experience being that the student athlete couldn't care less and is dying to run at the school that annually makes the NCAA Cross Country meet but is only offering 20%.

As a high school coach, I'd be deliriously happy if a much higher percentage of college coaches talked candidly with prospects about the amounts of athletic scholarship aid they are likely to be able to offer prospects. Absolutely, the actual amount will vary from prospect to prospect, but a simple disclaimer such as I've shown below could forestall no end of misunderstandings and ill feeling: "We bring in approximately twelve women per year on some form of athletic scholarship. We average 3.8 full scholarship equivalents per year and must distribute that amount among the roughly twelve individuals we bring in on scholarship each year. Another ten to twenty athletes come in each year as walk-ons, with no initial scholarship support, but with the prospect of earning such support as their performances merit. If you are a top-level prospect, this gives you some sort of idea of what level of support we might be able to bring you in on. Understand also that it's likely that the amount and timing of these individual award offers will vary somewhat based on the responses (accept/decline) of the highest level prospects that we recruit in any given year. If you are a high-achieving student, you may also come in line for assistance in the form of academic scholarships. For more information about academic scholarships, contact..."

Speaking of the differences between male and female prospects, it is not merely the supply-side of different numbers of scholarships available for men and women that drives the differences in awards. There's also a demand-side to this equation. A few years ago, a college coach (and it may have been Jay Johnson, but I can't say for sure) told me that if you talked to the top 50 finishers in the boys state cross country meet, you'd find out that 48 wanted to go on and run in college. If you talked to the top 50 finishers in the girls state cross country meet, you'd find out that 10 wanted to go on and run in college. I'm guessing that figure of 10 has risen some in the interim, but it's still true that a larger percentage of the guys than the girls nurture a strong desire to compete at the college level. The implication here, then, is that an expression of interest in running by the 40th-place girl at the state cross country meet is likely to grab a college recruiter's attention a lot more quickly than an expression of interest from the 40th-place boy. Even this year, I've heard of athletic scholarship offers being extended to girls who missed the top 100 (all classifications combined) of the Colorado state cross country meet; I feel safe in saying that opportunity would never arise for a boy finishing outside of the top 100.

*   *   *   *   *

College Recruiting: A Give and Take, Part IV – HS Coach
By Alan Versaw; February 24, 2008 (http://co,,milesplit.us/articles/21863)

I send college coaches and recruiting coordinators information about prospect athletes. I do it knowing that my e-mail messages are likely to be either promptly deleted or only skimmed over. I do it on the hope that it does genuine good every once in a while. I do it because I like to think I'd read those messages if the roles were reversed. I do it in hopes of building relationships with those charged with identifying and persuading prospective recruits. I do it out of reciprocity for all that the student-athletes have given me over the spans of their high school careers. So, what process do I try to follow when I have an athlete who is capable of competing at the collegiate level? Here's a brief summary:

1. In the spring of his/her junior year, at the latest, I check to see if there is interest in continuing to the collegiate level. If not, the process ends there. If there is indecision, we talk. If there is genuine interest, I ask them to identify some schools where they think they might be interested in running. Lately, I've added a brief form for them to fill out. It asks them to identify interests in terms of types of schools (large vs. small, private vs. state school, Christian vs. secular, high-profile programs vs. lower-profile programs, engineering vs. liberal arts, etc.) they are interested in attending. We discuss the levels of school (DI, DII, DIII, NAIA) for which the athlete's accomplishments merit consideration.

2. Later, we discuss their lists of potential schools. To the extent that I am competent in this area, we talk about what these schools can offer them academically. We discuss the advantages and disadvantages of training in climates different from what they are accustomed to. We look at rosters and

past results for these programs and try to identify how the competitive levels of the teams mesh with the students' goals and personalities. We look for clues regarding the personalities of the programs. Following this, I encourage them to make some sort of initial contact with the schools they are most interested in. Most frequently, they will fill out the prospective athlete questionnaire on the school's athletic web site. I'm increasingly of the opinion, however, that submitting this form serves only moderately well as an initial contact. Sometimes, our athletes have received calls from coaches the same day the form was submitted. More often, the athletes who complete these online forms never hear a thing.

3. Following the initial contact by the prospect, I send a brief, introductory e-mail about this individual to the coaches at the schools they have contacted. I didn't always do this in the past, but I do it now. I get a response to this e-mail somewhere around 40% of the time.

4. Assuming the individual in question shows some improvement in his/her senior cross country season (and we have an excellent record of our runners showing improvement as seniors), I will send out a second e-mail to the coach sometime late in the cross country season informing him/her of how things have progressed during the season. I get a response to this e-mail maybe a little over 10% of the time. As a part of both this e-mail and the previous e-mail, I invite the coach to get back to me with any questions they have about the prospect.

5. I encourage the prospect to maintain contact with the coaches at the schools they are interested in attending. Perhaps the most difficult issue prospects face is inquiring about the possibility of an official visit. I've just about concluded that official visits involving more than 50 miles of travel go only to the very highest tier of recruits. Personal humility is stressed from day one in our program and that message seems to resonate with almost all of our kids. Unfortunately (or maybe not-so-unfortunately), this translates into them being ill-at-ease with almost any form of self-promotion.

6. I urge all of my prospects to send notes of closure and appreciation to all who have recruited them once they do sign with a particular school. This is simply a matter of basic human civility. Many have done this before I prompted them to do it. If the coach/recruiter has sent me a response at any point in the season, I will send them a note at this time, too, thanking them for their efforts.

7. I derive no joy from confrontation, but I don't go out of my way to avoid it, either. I'm hardwired to take a stand rather than recede into the background. If a coach/recruiter is stringing a prospect along beyond National Letter of Intent Day, I will send a polite note asking them to play straight with the prospect. By this time, if not sooner, the coach/recruiter should have given any prospect they've been keeping contact with a clear statement of where they stand (One way of making a clear statement is to

truthfully tell them, "We need to wait and see what the responses of our first tier of recruits are before we know if we can make an offer. We expect to notify you by [insert a reasonably proximate date here]. "). If the recruiter or coach has not let the prospect know where he/she stands within a few days of the opening of the signing period, I will make a contact with that coach. I doubt this practice has won me many friends, but what I am asking for is simply a matter of courtesy. Treat others as you would have them treat you.

Okay, here are my opinions on the role of the HS coach in the recruiting process:

- The longer the coach has been coaching and the more college athletes they've coached the more their input/influence can be beneficial to both the student/family and the college coach/program.

- If the kid is really good and the coach is really young then 99% of the time the coaches ego is, at least in a small way, tied up in where the kid goes. Good news is that this young coach will soon, with more success, become the coach above. The bad news is they currently this young coach is a pain in the rear for the college coach and the can, potentially, get the kid and the family focused on the wrong variables.

- HS coaches know WAY MORE about this process than most HS guidance counselors. My story: I loved Mrs. Olsen, my counselor at DCHS, like a second mom yet she had no clue what a 4:25 1,600m runner should receive in the Big 8 Conference. The answer, of course, is nothing and the 27 ACT I had simply meant I was 0.2 lower than the "average" student at CU. No academic money, no athletic money... and the second best choice I ever made ;-).

- The kid should do the majority of the work in this process; if they can't, then I know that personally I don't want to coach them at the college level. Why? Well - and this is an extreme example - I won't be the coach who gets them out of their dorm room and walks them to class, though other college coaches, especially in other sports, view that as part of their job (and this happens on EVERY campus in the BCS schools in at least one sport). So, kids should send the initial emails, kids should follow up those emails with a voicemail, kids should walk their butt down to the counselors office and tell the administrative assistant, as nicely as they can, that they need their transcripts faxed to both the NCAA Clearinghouse and _____ schools. Of the 10-20% remaining the majority should be parents parenting - telling the kid they can't afford 40k a year but they can afford 15k a year - things like that. If those two things happen then the HS coach can do, in my humble opinion, the most important thing for their HS program: they can walk the halls, they can spy on the mile time trial in gym class or whatever good coaches do to recruit kids, maybe the next stud, to their program. The best HS distance programs in the country do two things: they make distance running cool, attracting better athletes (and yes, attracting them "away" from other sports) and they practice when others do not. The HS coaches I'm friends with let the kids and the parents do the majority of the work in the college recruiting process while they worry about their internal, on-site recruiting.

* * * * *

College Recruiting: A Give and Take, Part V – HS Coach

By Alan Versaw; February 28, 2008 (http://co,,milesplit.us/articles/22084)

It's pretty much a given that colleges will be clamoring over the Foot Locker finalists, the top 40 or so individuals at NXN, and many state champions. We, as high school coaches, typically don't need much help getting notice for the kids who happen to fall into one or more of these categories. The question for most of us is, "What to do for that athlete who is clearly good enough to run at some level of college competition but isn't necessarily at the level where he/she is hard not to notice?"

One thing that I think I've learned this year is that the college-bound student athlete should probably keep a few more irons in the fire than the typical college-bound student. High school seniors who have no intention of competing in college athletics probably don't need to apply to more than two or three schools, unless the schools they apply to are highly selective (think Stanford, Michigan, MIT, Ivy League, and the like). College-bound student-athletes probably should keep a few more options open. I think I'll start making that suggestion.

Why would the college-bound student-athletes want to keep more options open? I recently learned the hard way that even if a student is a good match for a school--academically, athletically, and socially--the school may not share that perspective and may not offer enough financial aid to sustain the pulse of the student's hopes and dreams. The coach at that school may decide they're already top-heavy in your student-athlete's best event and decide not to offer any scholarship assistance at all—at least not initially.

And, let's face it, for many athletically-inclined high school seniors, athletic accomplishment can be the ticket to getting into a school they could not otherwise afford. As long as I'm dealing with some athletes from families of modest means, this implies that it just might be worth keeping options alive at more than two or three schools.

If you're a high school coach and you call, text or email the kid in their first week as a college freshman on the campus of _____ then YOU have a problem and your problem is need, specifically the fact that YOU need something from the coach-athlete relationship that is unhealthy. You wanna' know what the kid's doing? I can tell you what the kid's doing. He/She thinks they have a ton in common with their roommate, a position that is will likely change come December and a position that will be laughable come March; the kid loves the fact that the opposite sex is living either on the floor above or the floor below**; they are scared of this afternoon's practice and they can't believe how much better EVERYONE on the team is than they are; if they are a distance runner they are petrified of the fact that the "easy" run they went on yesterday was harder and faster then their HS coach's 5x1,000m workouts; they can't get their mother to stop with the "but the room is so small - are you going to be alright, honey?"

...so in the midst of that first week of college what the heck are you doing calling them? Obviously, I don't know WHY you are calling them, but I do know what your call is doing to the poor kid. You're confusing the kid because your voice is familiar and comforting while all of the other stimuli around them is some combination of: new, exciting, scary, uncomfortable, hard. You're inhibiting the growth they will likely experience from being thrown out of their comfort zone, a comfort zone that likely included being successful in school and successful in track, two things they aspire to at this new level but two things that, in the first week of school, appear unattainable.

They will adapt. They like you. They don't need you.

*   *   *   *   *

College Recruiting: A Give and Take, Part VI – HS to College
By Alan Versaw; March 4, 2008 (http://co,,milesplit.us/articles/22072)

1. Tell kids to wrap their minds around new numbers:

- In college, athletes on the track will run the 1,500m and the 3,000m, not the 1,600m and 3,200m. If the kid has a great race in their conference indoor 3,000m as a freshman they likely came through the first 1,600m FASTER than they ran the 1,600m as junior. For example, I ran 4:40 for 1,600m as a junior and though I ran that in the Denver area (5,200 ft.) it still only converts to 4:33-4:34 1,600m at sea level; I ran 8:22 as a freshman in the Big 8 3,000m which is about 4:27-4:28 1,600m pace.

- Similarly, at the Division I level the way you qualify for outdoor nationals is to hit a regional qualifying performance. Then you go to one of four NCAA DI regional meets and if you perform well you advance. The regional standard for the women's 5,000m run is 16:52, which is roughly 5:26 per 1,600m and roughly 10:52 for 3,200m. I haven't been to a HS meet in a while, but I'm going to say that the 10:52 girl does pretty well in most meets in most states (California the first big exception that comes to mind), yet she has to maintain that pace for 4.5 more laps just to get into the NCAA DI Regional meet, let alone be competitive in that meet.

- For most kids, their long run in HS will become a distance that they will run 3-4 times a week; thus, by the time they come home for winter break their old "easy day loop" is way too short for their new easy day and they might simply run it twice to get the appropriate stimulus. Big change.

2. Athlete: When the college coach sends you your summer instructions do the following:

- Read it; sleep one night. Read it again; sleep another night.

- Read it again and email the coach 3 questions about what they've written. In this email ask only questions that directly relate to the training guidelines they sent you. Do not ask how many quarters you'll need for the laundry machine in the dorm or any other question

your parents are curious about. Tell the coach you have read their training guidelines three times and that you're writing to make sure you do not misinterpret the guidelines and that you make smooth training transition.

3. Parents and HS Coaches: Let the kid do most of the dumb things they did when they got the offer to compete at _____ college/university.

- Brent Vaughn ran fast in HS for 3,200m, something under 8:50. I called him this morning and asked, "How many times a week did you eat fast food spring of your senior year, when you ran well?" Though he took his lunch once a week, he admitted that most weekends he had at least one fast food meal, so he settled on 5-6 times a week. I do not condone this, but I do think that if his HS coach or his parents had tried to help him change his diet the summer prior to college it would be counter-productive. Suggestion #1 above will scare any kid who truly wants to be good, which should translate into doing everything they can to be prepared from a training standpoint, yet if the kid was fueled by fast food the past 3 years don't change that - it's simply too many variables to try to change at one time.

- This is not the summer for the kid to do a lot of new things - if they simply do the same things they've done previous summers, while following an anal (yes, anal) interpretation of the training guidelines sent by their new coach, they'll likely enter college excited, refreshed and ready for the challenges I discussed in part 5.

* * * * *

College Recruiting: A Give and Take, Part VII – Wrap-Up
By Alan Versaw; March 8, 2008 (http://co,,milesplit.us/articles/22165)

Here's what I'd suggest: During the summer between your junior and senior year of high school, go to the official athletic web site for every school you think you might be interested in attending. Then, identify three to five more schools at about the same competitive level and go to their sites as well. If your interests span schools at different competitive levels, do the analysis below separately for each level—the reasons for this will become apparent as you read on. Once you're at a school's site, go to the Track and Field page. If you're a distance runner, you can go to the Cross Country page and find a shorter list of names to sort through. Then go to the team roster. Carefully note the names and classes of athletes of your gender and your specialty area on the roster. Now, go back through previous rosters. In some cases, you can simply find previous year's rosters by selecting from a drop box at the top of the roster page. With other programs, you will need to click on "Archives" to look at previous year's rosters.

Go back two, three, four, and five years and examine closely what proportion of the incoming athletes from each year stayed with the program. Especially note how many freshmen continued with the program their sophomore year, but—for more complete information—track freshman to junior year as well.

Calculate a retention rate for each school and coach you're interested in competing for. Do the same for the 3 – 5 additional schools at roughly the same competitive level. If this information is not available at the web site, you are not out-of-bounds to ask for it politely. Don't jump to conclusions yet. You must first understand that no school ever had a 100% athlete retention rate. And sometimes an athlete leaves a school for academic reasons rather than athletic reasons. Although you're used to thinking of a 65% as a D, that is—in many cases—an excellent retention rate. Finally, bear in mind that retention rates are typically higher for men than women (yet another reason why, in any given year, a school will almost certainly have more available track and field scholarships for women than for men).

Having acknowledged all that, it is now time to compare across schools. Let's say that you're looking at six different schools. The freshman-to-junior retention rate for athletes of your gender and specialty over the last five years at these schools are, hypothetically: 60%, 70%, 40%, 30%, 70%, and 50%. Note that these percentages will vary somewhat depending on how competitive the schools you're looking at are.

Now, what should these numbers tell you? The numbers should be sending up red flags for the schools at the lower end of the spectrum of whatever grouping of schools you're looking at. On the other hand, in this example, I'd be feeling pretty good about the schools scoring out at 70%. There are reasons why schools competing at roughly the same level show differing retention rates. Ignore these reasons at your own peril.

In fairness, if you're truly interested in pursuing one or more of the schools with lower retention rates in your target group, you should pose the question directly to the coach, "I looked at athlete retention rates for similar programs and your retention rate is lower than other schools I'm considering. Could you address that concern for me?" This gives the coach a chance to explain what might possibly be unusual circumstances. It allows you to take in information from another perspective before making your decision.

Understand that, should you pose this question, the coach—assuming he/she responds—will make an attempt to put the best possible spin on the question, but it's valuable to hear the coach out nevertheless. If you ask the question in person, you can pretty well nullify the non-response option. In either case, be alarmed if you sense your question being redirected. Understand also that, if you ask the question in a hostile tone, you likely just torched your scholarship chances at that school.

There is one major point I want to make as we wrap up this series, but first I want to reinforce the importance of Alan's suggestion. Very few families take the time to research the programs they're interested in, yet for the past 5-6 years every college program's web site has, just as Alan pointed out, an archive to the past 3-4 years results and rosters. And while Alan is right on about looking at retention rates I would add something that is as important, if not more important. Which athletes got better in the programs you're considering? Does this program have athletes who had similar PRs to me who are now running at a high level? These are simple questions and while it will take a few hours to go through the athlete bios for 2-3 programs and their results for the past few years, this is an important step that most families fail to take. We're all busy and we all wish we had more time; what I'm suggesting will take some time, but you'll be well served having gone through this exercise as you'll have a clear picture as to the question, "Do most athletes improve in this program?" Also, wait until you have your list narrowed down to 2-3 schools before you do this as this really would be a waste of time if you're starting the process with a list of 6 programs.

The final issue I want to raise is a question I think every senior in HS should be able to answer, "What do you need from your college coach?" This is a simple question, but the reason I bring it up as part of this "transition from HS to college training" section is that many college freshman expect their new college coach to be a similar version of their HS coach and that their college coach will do the same things as their HS coach did for them.

While the differences between the two coaches are numerous and while both the college coach and the HS coach are, at the core of their respective job descriptions, educators, let me throw out the biggest difference between the two. In many situations, the college track coach will lose their job if their program either fails to perform athletically, or in some cases fails to perform academically. 99% of HS track coaches will not lose their job as a teacher if their track program stinks, nor does the school keep separate academic performance records for the HS students who choose to participate in track and field. In one setting, athletic and academic performance is the primary issue while in the other participation is the primary issue.

One other tip, when you arrive on campus you should be willing to learn by observation, watching - even mirroring - the successful upperclassmen on the team to see how this whole thing works. After 2-3 days of careful observation you will no doubt have a question; go into the college coaches office (mornings are usually best) and ask one simple question. It might be, "I know that we stretch during practice, yet I'm wondering if there is any other supplemental stretching I'm supposed to doing during the day or on the weekends?" That may not be the best example of a question, yet that question shows that you're paying attention during practice, but it also shows that you want to learn your new coaches system, down to the small details such as supplemental stretching to support your training load.